Giving Our Children a Fighting Chance

Poverty, Literacy, and the Development of Information Capital

Giving Our Children a Fighting Chance

Poverty, Literacy, and the
Development of Information Capital

Susan B. Neuman
Donna C. Celano

Teachers College, Columbia University
New York and London

Published by Teachers College Press, 1234 Amsterdam Avenue, New York, NY 10027

Library of Congress Cataloging-in-Publication Data

Neuman, Susan B.
　　Giving our children a fighting chance : poverty, literacy, and the development of information capital / Susan B. Neuman and Donna C. Celano.
　　　p. cm.
　　Includes bibliographical references and index.
　　ISBN 978-0-8077-5358-3 (pbk. : alk. paper)
　　ISBN 978-0-8077-5359-0 (hardcover : alk. paper)
　　　1. Literacy–Social aspects–Pennsylvania–Philadelphia–Case studies.
　　2. Libraries and community–Pennsylvania–Philadelphia–Case studies.
　　3. Educational equalization–Pennsylvania–Philadelphia–Case studies.
　　4. Philadelphia (Pa.)–Social conditions–Case studies. 5. Chestnut Hill
　　(Philadelphia, Pa.) I. Celano, Donna. II. Title.
　　LC153.P45N48　2012
　　302.2'2440974811–dc23　　　　　　　　　　　　　　　　2012020743

ISBN 978-0-8077-5358-3 (paperback)
ISBN 978-0-8077-5359-0 (hardcover)

Printed on acid-free paper
Manufactured in the United States of America

19　18　17　16　15　14　13　12　　　　　8　7　6　5　4　3　2　1

To the Free Library—
the gift to the city of Philadelphia that keeps on giving

Contents

Acknowledgments   ix

Introduction: The Ecology of Inequality   1

1. Same City, Different Paths   9

2. On the Streets Where They Live   22

3. The Paradox of the Level Playing Field   38

4. The New Work, The New Play   58

5. The More, the More (the Less, the Less)   76

6. The New Literacies   92

7. Developing Information Capital   105

8. Conclusions   120

Postscript: Breaking Out—
Giving Our Children a Fighting Chance   131

Appendix   145

References   151

Index   156

About the Authors   164

Acknowledgments

We owe our deep gratitude to so many individuals over the years who contributed to our efforts. First and foremost, we would like to thank Richard Cox, former vice president of the William Penn Foundation, whose vision and foresight helped to create the comprehensive community-based initiative that supported the modern urban library system in Philadelphia. He and his foundation were committed to closing the gap between disadvantaged and advantaged children through greater access to resources and information. We are also extremely grateful to Ken Finkel at the foundation who was central in helping us get this project off the ground. During the course of our conversations there were many times we encouraged them to be more public about their grant-giving activities to the city, and the tremendous benefits that accrued from these efforts. Their response to us was to let their good works speak for themselves. We hope that this book provides some evidence of their incredible dedication and commitment to improving the lives of children and adults in Philadelphia.

We could not have conducted this work without the support of two giants in the field of library services. Elliot Shelkrot, former director of the Free Library, was an impassioned supporter of branch libraries and their promise for providing free and equal access to information resources to the neighborhoods in Philadelphia. Hedra Packman, head of Children's Library Services, made it all work. One of the foremost leaders in community library services, she worked tirelessly, along with her colleague Theresa Ramos, to ensure that Philadelphia's children receive the benefits of every grant opportunity from homework help to summer programs, to technology innovations and special programs. These women stand alone in their determination, grace, and dedication to children.

We wish to thank the wonderful librarians and LEAP leaders at the Lillian Marrero and Chestnut Hill libraries. Librarians Sara Palmer at Lillian Marrero and Kate Bowman-Johnston at Chestnut Hill were infinitely gracious and always willing to answer our questions throughout our work. LEAP leaders Elaine Kumpf and Dunia Kravchak, as well, helped us learn about the neighborhoods and after-school programs. Watching them interact with students, while always maintaining their sense of humor and delight in their work, was a pleasure to observe.

This type of field work could not have been conducted without our able and talented research team. We would like to thank William McKinney, Joseph Gonzales, Samantha Longdin, Sam Pack, Hannah Ashley, and Rachel Stern, our urban ethnographers for their very careful and detailed observations. We benefited tremendously from Mary Hickert Herring, ethnographer extraordinaire, for her impressive knowledge of Philadelphia and its neighborhoods. In addition, we are especially grateful to Jeremy Sparig, visual ethnographer, who seemed to be able to capture the essence of an observation with his camera. His work is shown throughout the book.

We also appreciate our friends and colleagues who reviewed previous drafts and chapters of the book. Colleagues Tanya Wright, Ashley Pinkham, Tanya Kaefer, and Andrea Pampaloni willingly gave of their time to provide insightful comments. Colleagues in policy, business, research, and practice helped us to view our work from many different perspectives and gave us much food for thought. We would like to thank Richard Rothstein, Marie McCormick, Liz Alperin Solms, Noreen O'Neill, and Dean Rosencranz, as well as our anonymous reviewers, for their very thorough and perceptive comments.

Finally, we thank our greatest fans, Russell and Mike, who were always willing to listen to one more story, and one more draft. They continued to encourage us throughout the many years of data collection and reflection and we are forever grateful for their inspiration and support.

Giving Our Children a Fighting Chance

Poverty, Literacy, and the
Development of Information Capital

The Ecology of Inequality

Like a bright beacon on the hill, the Lillian Marrero public library rises majestically above the deserted buildings and bulldozed voids below on Germantown Avenue. Here in the heart of what is known as the Philadelphia Badlands, makeshift garbage dumps line the sidewalks. The tall grass that surrounds abandoned lots does nothing to obscure the stacks of tires, worn stuffed chairs, and piles of bottles, bags, and take-out containers indicative of the profound decline in the economy of this part of the city since its heyday in the mid-20th century. Although it's a stunningly beautiful summer day, one that normally would draw you outdoors, there's not a seat to be had in the library. By 10:15 a.m., you can hear the hum of dozens of people speaking in hushed tones, groups gathered around the computers, and some 40 others scattered throughout the library, browsing the stacks or reading quietly at one of its nine tables. Every 15 minutes or so, a library staff member sweeps through the room tucking in the vacated chairs, picking up trash and discarded books, and readying the room for the continuing onslaught of new patrons.

Grabbing the #23 bus, and traveling just 6.6 miles from the Badlands, you'll find a strikingly similar scene at the graceful Chestnut Hill library, next to the old trolley turnaround. Its front doors are located only 20 feet from the same busy two-lane Germantown Avenue, but its tiny carefully tended gardens inside the wrought-iron fence and under a canopy of century-old shade trees gives it the feel of a sylvan oasis far removed from traffic. Inside, here too, the library is bustling with about 20 adults, either at the computers or selecting books. On this fine warm day, more than 20 preschoolers are cuddled along an architect's replica of a trolley filled with benches and murals that hearkens back to the day when trolleys were the primary means of public transit on this Avenue.

"CUT"—AN ENTERPRISING YOUNG VIDEOGRAPHER might say at this point, for this is where the parallels end. Although there are remarkable similarities in the number of people who use these libraries, the nature of the activities within them could not look more different. There is Aquanette at the Lillian Marrero library, who is struggling to use the computer, looking for Section 8 housing after being told that she must vacate her residence

immediately. There is Christian, totally engrossed in reading the *Hazardous Material Endorsement Renewal Manual*, hoping to renew his commercial driver's license from the Pennsylvania State Department of Transportation. Several pages of copious notes by his side offer evidence of just how seriously he takes his study, while a thick pamphlet, "Purgatory and Prayer," hints at what sustains him. There is Michelle, watching her only child Theo play on the computer, recognizing that her own computer illiteracy will limit the potential for academic achievement of her unusually inquisitive child. Regardless of the specifics, their stories take on a saddening refrain: Our society has failed to school these young adults.

In the Chestnut Hill library, the contrast could not be more stark. There is the mother dutifully looking for guided leveled readers, coaching her 6-year-old son so that he's ready to zip right through to grade level 3. There's little 2-year-old Phoebe whose mother can't seem to resist giving an informal vocabulary lesson while she reads a story: "It says he has a puzzled expression. What do you think 'puzzled' means?" And there is Beth with her two children in tow, grabbing the latest John Sandfords and John Archers mysteries for herself along with a couple of books by Peggy Rathmann and Judith Viorst, which apparently are always winners with her young girls.

The underpinnings of desperation so palpable in the Lillian Marrero library result from a confluence of circumstances hardly imaginable by their Chestnut Hill counterparts: Poverty. Segregation. Environments where joblessness and lost hope are the norm. While many of us may vaguely recognize the ghettoization of poverty, few can appreciate how it concentrates environments that are progressively isolated geographically, socially, economically, and educationally.

Today, for example, a majority of urban Black residents in Philadelphia will live under conditions of racial isolation so extreme that they satisfy the criteria of hyper-segregation—places where Blacks are highly segregated on multiple geographic dimensions simultaneously (Massey, 2007). Discrimination against Latinos is hardly less virulent. Whereas in 1989 Hispanics were 19% *less likely* than Blacks to experience adverse treatment in residential markets, in 2000 they were 8% *more likely* to suffer such discrimination (Mason, 2004). Extensive *linguistic profiling* in metropolitan areas along with increasing anti-immigration fervor has only intensified the effects of such residential segregation (Ryan, 2010).

Exacerbating these conditions is yet a newer form of segregation—this one based on class (Reardon, 2011). Over the last 20 years, demographer Douglas Massey and his colleagues (Massey, Gross, & Eggers, 1991) have reported astonishing increases in the degree of residential segregation. Designating families earning incomes below the federal poverty line for a family of four as poor, and those earning incomes more than four times above the poverty level as affluent, he reports increases in class segregation by more than 50%. Those with money are more likely to live in homogeneously privileged neighborhoods like Chestnut Hill, interacting almost exclusively with other affluent people. Those without money are increasingly confined to homogeneously poor neighborhoods like the Badlands, yielding a density of material deprivation that is unprecedented in our history.

It is this hardening of the class stratification system, as poverty and privilege grow ever more geographically concentrated, that significantly impedes social mobility. It creates a set of mutually reinforcing patterns that more or less institutionalize one's class position, a set of patterns closely linked to one's education and, even more closely, with one's literacy skills: Children from low-income families with poorly educated parents, little experience reading books, and multiple social problems will end up in schools with the fewest resources and the most inexperienced teachers to help them learn. On the other hand, children from affluent families with well-educated parents and extensive experiences with books and reading, attend high-achieving schools with the finest and most well-paid teachers that are in the best position to promote learning. In short, the spatial concentration of poverty and affluence—in this case within the same school district—virtually guarantees the intergenerational transmission of class position. Poor children don't have a chance to succeed. Rich children have little option not to.

You can see how this social geography works against human capital formation at the Lillian Marrero library in the Badlands. Reynaldo, a young Latino man, 22 and out of work, spends time at the library every day trying to learn more about anime, a form of film animation that originated in Japan. He dreams of being a film director or a screenwriter, an interest he developed thanks to his English teacher in middle school. But due to family problems he dropped out of school in 11th grade. Now he finds himself without the skills or the connections to qualify for even an entry-level position. He says that he might work on his GED in the fall, but his furtive glances at the door plainly indicate that he would rather not talk about his future.

Chris, 25, also a regular at the library, enjoys the quiet air-conditioned setting to support his interest in poetry—mostly Langston Hughes. He also studiously works on learning another language, and occasionally uses the Rosetta Stone software on the library's computer. But he, too, dropped out of school. "I enjoyed math at one point, then it all fell apart." As he describes his experience at the local high school, the brightness in his eyes now dims. Until now, Chris had been sitting tall, leaning slightly forward, animated in describing his interests. Now he leans back and slumps down, his body language divulging volumes.

It would be easy to attribute Reynaldo and Chris's problems to some personality or dispositional factors; they were irresponsible, lazy, or lacked the desire to excel in school. Such designations reflect a characteristic feature in social psychology known as the *fundamental attribution error* (Ross, 1977), the general tendency for people to overestimate individual factors and underestimate situational factors. But the very fact that we see them and their friends daily at the *library,* not at a bar or a pool hall, indicates that the situational characteristic which has produced this hourglass economic structure is at work. It is not that Reynaldo and Chris have few aspirations; it is that neither has been born into a social position with the resources that could give them a fighting chance.

Resources come in a variety of forms. They may be material, such as income; emotional, such as love and family stability; or symbolic, such as prestige and social standing. Paradoxically, it is often the nonmaterial resources like social and cultural capital that carry the greatest potential for inequality (Putnam, 2000). Social capital relates to your social standing, the informal networks of friends and colleagues that you can draw upon for any kinds of tangible benefits. For example, you might learn about an upcoming but unadvertised position through the "grapevine," or find out what company might offer opportunities to get ahead with higher income or greater prestige. Moreover, within your circle of contacts, there develops a set of cultural practices that act as identifiers of your class membership. You might attend the same elite colleges, send your children to the same private schools, or buy the same foreign cars. Cultural capital in some ways acts like a secret handshake, defining your social group. Those with cultural capital, for example, will find ways to get their child the "best" teacher in the "best" school, influencing all those around them to get things done. They seem to know how to navigate the various power structures with confidence. They believe in themselves and expect achievement.

But as important as these resources are, the forces of computerization and market expansion have brought on yet another intangible resource, one that might trump all others: the rise of information capital. Today, the prosperity of companies and nations has come to demand high-level human and information capital—knowledge workers—who can mobilize their skills and talents to promote innovation and greater productivity (Levy & Murnane, 2004). As the newest form of human capital, information is seen as having an intrinsic value in and of itself; further, sharing information can be a means of sharing power. China, India, and Russia, for example, have expanded postgraduate education to 30 million students, almost double the numbers for the United States, to fill knowledge-intensive industries in their own developing economies (Jones, 2008). And what is true about today's rising skill needs will be even truer tomorrow as the pressure to compete and expand into specialized global markets increase, forcing knowledge workers toward even higher stakes characterized by innovation, artistry, out-of-the-box thinking.

Information capital is comprised of two modes of reasoning. The first and most common mode is knowledge-based (Hirsch, 1987). This sort of reasoning is rapid, extensive, and automatic, and powerfully evolves as the cumulative product of a person's experiences with words and the concepts to which they refer. The second mode of reasoning is conscious and rule-based, and involves logical, analytic thought (Bereiter, 2002). Both forms of information capital accrue through firsthand and secondhand experiences. Young children frequently acquire knowledge about the world through first-hand experience. Everyday play activities and conversations with adults and their peers provide many initial opportunities for knowledge-building. However, much of the information they will need as they grow older will not be available through conversations and experience. They will need to rely on a second source of information: print. In fact, cultural anthropologists and historians have long argued that reading represents a unique interface with the environment, providing access to the cumulative wisdom and knowledge built by current and previous generations (Scribner & Cole, 1973).

Reading has cognitive consequences that extend beyond the immediate task of understanding particular texts. Although many used to think that knowledge is merely a proxy for intellectual ability, recent evidence has shown that knowledge is highly related to the amount of reading (Cunningham & Stanovich, 1998). Studies have shown, for example, that as a primary source of information, students who are likely to read a lot, know a lot; those who are reluctant readers are likely to read less, and know less (Stanovich, 1986). In short, avid readers–regardless of general ability–tend to know more than those who read little, demonstrating what reading does for the mind. Further, these consequences are reciprocal and exponential in nature. Those who know a lot are likely to learn a lot more, faster; in other words, knowledge begets more knowledge (Willingham, 2006). This is a stunning finding because it means that children who get off to a fast start in reading are more likely to read more over the years; further, this very act of reading can develop vocabulary, general knowledge, and build information capital. Consequently, children's earliest experiences with print will establish a trajectory of learning that is cumulative over time–spiraling either upward or downward, carrying profound implications for the development of information capital.

This book describes how the contrasting ecologies of affluence and poverty contribute to disparities in the development of information capital. It begins early on with the differential access to exposure to print. It develops through parental supports that either nurture children's early independence or their intense involvement in print. These patterns are reified and compounded as their social worlds diverge, creating radical differences in parental expectations, access to knowledge, experiences, and attitudes toward learning prior to entering the school doors. As the digital age takes hold, it does not diminish but merely accelerates the divide, exacerbating the earlier advantages for some students who have come to use the technology for the creation of new knowledge and the manipulation of information.

Our laboratory for understanding these extremes of inequality, paradoxically, has been the neighborhood library. You might think it a curious choice. Carnegie libraries, after all, represent the very symbol of our country's commitment to equality, to lifelong learning, to free and equal access to information. Yet it is in these settings, where people have the freedom to come and go as they wish, that we could develop an acute sense of the juxtaposition of geographically concentrated wealth and poverty and how this new ecological order might contribute to educational inequality. For over 10 years–roughly 1998 to 2009–our research team examined the development of information capital, conducting observations and interviews, following story hours and special events. We walked every block in each neighborhood to better understand how the physical environment played a role in children's development and preparation for schooling. We counted every logographic sign, and spent time in public places to examine how print was used in the neighborhood and how children might be developing as young readers. Given the demands that reading imposes, we observed how teens and young adults transitioned from learning to read to reading to learn, using reading in the service of finding things out and knowing. And finally, recognizing how computerization has greatly altered reading and writing, we examined its use not only in the libraries themselves but in their communities as well.

Using this ecological perspective, this book tells the story of two Philadelphia neighborhoods, one of poverty and one of privilege. Our research context is the neighborhood public library, but the story is not about libraries. Rather, it is about how information capital develops, and the contributing resources that provide either a dearth or an abundance of resources for its formation. Chapter 1 sets the stage for analysis, providing readers with our theoretical framework, our research context, and the purpose of our analysis. Chapter 2 describes the differences in early access to print for young children in these neighborhoods. Chapter 3 begins to detail the basic paradox that has often flummoxed policymakers and educators. It argues that even when we "level the playing field"–therefore creating equal access to material resources–we still have an unleveled playing field, suggesting that other factors, namely scaffolding adults, may make the difference in children's literacy lives. Chapter 4 then moves to the promise of new technology for closing the gap, and finds that the early patterns set by parental interactions in reading have profound effects on how children use digital technology. Chapter 5 records the beginnings of the transition from learning to read to reading to learn for tweens, and it is here that we begin to record the growing knowledge gap. In Chapter 6, as students become aware of the capabilities of these new media, the disparities increase, leading some students to move toward using the medium for information purposes, and others entertainment. In Chapter 7, we argue that discrepancies in resources have further diverged so that some children are using the media to develop expertise, demonstrating their increasing use of media for information capital. In Chapter 8, we sum up, highlighting our conclusions, before turning to policy implications–both immediate and in the long term.

The end result is that the intensification of class status has given rise to a new set of self-reinforcing mechanisms that have deepened unequal access to information capital. Class status, intensified by increasing geographic concentrations in urban communities, has further accelerated the Matthew Effect, the maxim of the rich get richer and the poor get poorer. It has created a knowledge gap which has a far more detrimental effect on social mobility and educational opportunity. Without serious and far-reaching educational and societal reforms, as we describe in our postscript, students who live in concentrated poverty will not have a fighting chance.

Chestnut Hill

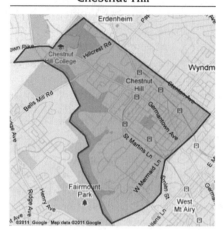

Philadelphia Badlands

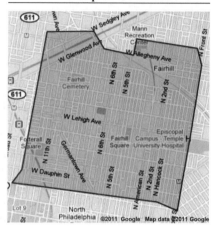

The Two Philadelphia Neighborhoods and the Road That Connects Them (Germantown Avenue)

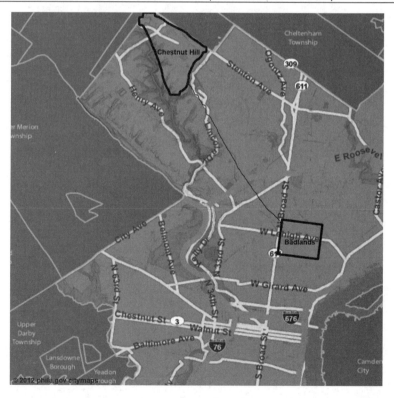

CHAPTER 1

Same City, Different Paths

"Picture Perfect" is how you might describe the gentrified neighborhood of Chestnut Hill. As you stroll down Germantown Avenue, the community's main thoroughfare, you will find a streetscape that is beautifully maintained and full of pedestrians enjoying it. Teams of families stroll the sidewalks with their babies and children ride their bikes as older residents visit their favorite haunts. The quaint mile-long business strip along the tree-lined main street is home to a range of stores—everything from an independent pharmacy and a shoe repair, to art galleries, day spas, Oriental rug specialists, antique dealers, boutiques of all kinds, jewelers, restaurants, banks, and much more. The sidewalks and streets are swept clear of debris, expensively wrought metal waste receptacles are emptied before they get full, and meticulously designed window boxes, sidewalk planters, and hanging baskets add a homey splash of color.

Much has changed here since the 18th century, when Chestnut Hill, with its lush greenery and wide open spaces, first served as a summer vacation spot for many wealthy Center City Philadelphia families. In 1854 the Chestnut Hill Railroad opened, making an easy commute to and from the center of town. From the mid-19th century through today, the neighborhood has served as the functional equivalent of a "railroad suburb," although it is technically part of the city. Starting around 1880, wealthy families moved in, commissioning Philadelphia's most prominent architects to build grand, stately residences.

While the local coffee shop is now a Starbucks, and the trolley that ran up Germantown Avenue has been replaced by a bus (still a sore subject with some local residents), the area has the same look and feel of affluence as it did 100 years ago. A wide variety of 19th- and early 20th-century residential buildings have been preserved, owned nowadays by attorneys, business executives, and other professionals. Shady side streets contain a large number of neat, well-kept row houses, accommodating many singles and young families.

Because it is geographically isolated from the rest of the city by the Wissahickon Creek and the meandering Fairmount Park on its western border and pastures to the north, Chestnut Hill has become known as the "suburb within the city." The 19118 zip code has considerable cache, and is almost entirely coterminous with its cultural boundaries. Its charm is recognized outside of the region—in 2007, Forbes.com designated Chestnut Hill as one of seven "top urban enclaves" in the nation. Although a growing number of professional African American and Hispanic families have moved into the area, with a fair number of recent immigrants from South America and Eastern Europe, nearly 80% of the population is White.

With wealth, as they say, comes privileges. And a child growing up in this community would have a hard time not garnering much of its riches. The baby's parents probably enjoy a substantial income and live in a comfortable house—Chestnut Hill boasts the highest average income in the city at $110,000, as well as the highest average housing prices (nearly $400,000 in 2008). Both are likely to be well-educated (nearly 95% of the population has graduated from high school and 63% has attained a bachelor's degree) and will work in a profession. Quite often, the mother—or increasingly the father—will drop out of the workforce to raise the child during the early years. Child care centers and preschools are plentiful and vie for parents' attention, including Montessori, Reggio Emilia, as well as specialty play-based programs that integrate the martial arts in their academic programs. The parent might also choose to attend one of the baby enrichment classes offered in the area: music classes at an area church, gymnastic classes at the recreation center, story time at the local library. As the child grows older, the plethora of after-school activities is overwhelming. A copy of the community newspaper, *The Chestnut Hill Local,* features a wide array: soccer, T-ball, and basketball; violin lessons; drama classes.

When the child reaches school age, many parents here will face a difficult choice: should the child attend the local public school, or go to one of the many prestigious private schools in the area? Neither choice is a bad one, really; both feature experienced staff, up-to-date curricula, and plentiful resources. There's the stately kindergarten through grade 8 public school—John Story Jencks—located in the heart of the community. In 2009 on the state tests, over 90% of the students scored proficient or higher in math and 80% scored proficient or higher in reading; numbers approximately 40% above the city norm. Parents may also choose from one of the many private schools with such tony names as Chestnut Hill Academy or the exclusive Springside School. The library in one of these private school holds more than 10,000 books. On the weekends, parents might visit historic Pastorious Park for a concert, hike in nearby Fairmount Park, stroll among the gardens at the Morris Arboretum, or hit the courts or links at the Philadelphia Cricket Club. Summers, as well, offer what parents here would call worthwhile activities: specialty camps running the gamut from archery to yoga, combined with family trips and vacations all to keep the little ones engaged. Come

**A Street in
Chestnut Hill**

high school, conversations in this neighborhood often turn to where (not if!) to attend college, aided by advice from experienced college counselors and legacy family and friends.

Inviting and calm, pleasant and clean, it's tempting to stay and hang out for a while in one of Chestnut Hill's outdoor cafés. The determined traveler, however, has only to catch the bus down Germantown Avenue and ride for a while over the original cobblestone-paved streets. Within a 20-minute bus ride, you soon come to another world. You swiftly move to a community that shares much in common with Chestnut Hill—the same city, the same elected officials, the same police force, the same school district—but one that is light-years away.

Here, as we turn off Germantown Avenue onto Allegheny Avenue, is the heart of the Philadelphia Badlands. Again we find historic buildings, but the once-grand churches and residences are now skeletons of their former grandeur. Desolation is everywhere: row houses along the avenue and on side streets are boarded up. A large school stands abandoned. Graffiti adorns high walls. The few businesses operating here close their doors early each day, shuttered behind high iron gates.

A View of the
Philadelphia
Badlands

It wasn't always like this. At about the same time wealthy families were building mansions in Chestnut Hill, this area emerged as a thriving commercial center. During the late 1800s and early 1900s, jobs abounded in the many factories here. Harwick and Magee operated a large carpet mill at 7th and Lehigh. The world-famous Stetson Hat company had a sprawling complex at 5th and Montgomery, a 12-acre site employing more than 5,500 people and offering an infirmary, a library, and a parlor for evening social events. Lehigh Avenue was busy, dotted by local shops, impressive churches, and outstanding schools.

As early as the 1930s, though, things began to change. Some businesses started to move south. After World War II, much of the area's Caucasian population moved to surrounding suburbs, lured by affordable, new housing. In the 1950s the first Puerto Rican workers started to arrive, aided by efforts of the New Jersey Growers Association in collaboration with the U.S. Employment Service.

These migrants found what historian Carmen Whalen (2001) has called "a plethora of limited opportunities"–jobs in a secondary job market that offered low pay, poor working conditions, little security, and few avenues for advancement. Many of these early Latino settlers worked primarily in manufacturing jobs, such as the cigarette, candy, and garment industries; or had service jobs in hotels and restaurants.

As "White flight" took over and more long-term residents left the area, Hispanic and African American families started to move in. Tensions flared among the different racial groups. The area's economic conditions continued to decline and by the 1970s abandoned factories marred the neighborhood. The manufacturing jobs were gone for good. The Stetson Hat factory, once the largest employer in the city, closed in 1971, and its building was gone by 1977, either demolished or destroyed by fire. Blight followed the loss of the neighborhood's economic base. Homes were abandoned; drugs, violence, and high dropout rates began to plague the area.

The resulting isolation and poverty has taken a toll on this once proud area. Today, families strolling down Lehigh Avenue face what looks like a war zone. Although community gardens provide a bit of green in a bleak landscape, for the most part the struggle, *la lucha*, remains. Trash is everywhere: mounding up on sidewalks, floating across streets, and hiding under cars. Young men hang out on street corners brazenly selling their drugs. Sometimes you glimpse a small bag being clutched, ready for a handoff. Colorful murals painted on the sides of buildings memorialize slain dealers. Even the most Goliath-like efforts to clean up the drug trade have fallen far short of their goals.

While Chestnut Hill remains geographically isolated from the rest of the city, the Badlands stand apart as well, but not solely because of their physical boundaries. Unlike Chestnut Hill, the boundaries are amorphous and somewhat disputed, though it's generally agreed to include the 25th precinct. In Chestnut Hill, a lush finger of Fairmount Park sets the area apart; here economic and social disparities are the real barriers.

No one quite knows how the Philadelphia Badlands got its name. Some say it refers to the high concentration of the Irish mob and, subsequently, for more recent street gang activities of African Americans and Puerto Ricans (Goode & Schneider, 1994). Others say it's the nickname the cops gave to this four-square mile section of North Philly during the heyday of "Operation Sunrise," a massive effort by police, state troopers, and federal agents to reclaim the neighborhood from the drug dealers who perpetuated violence on the local citizens. Still others say the term was popularized by former Philadelphia news reporter Steve Lopez in his book *Third and Indiana* (1994). In modern Philadelphia, all agree that the Badlands can be as hostile as the old frontier, with modern-day outlaws still ruling the open-air drug markets.

Raising a child in the Badlands is a challenge for parents. Gang activity among the Irish (who represent about 12% of the community), African Americans, and Latinos (the majority in this part of the city), is constant.

Communication among groups often breaks down. About 53% of the families speak English at home, while 46% speak Spanish as their primary language. Coinciding with the inevitable racial segregation and discrimination, children face an even greater challenge: poverty. Nearly all children born here live in households below the poverty line. In the Fairhill neighborhood, to the north of Allegheny Avenue, family income is the lowest in the city, dropping from around $27,000 in 1991 to less than $18,000 in 2005–2006. The adjacent neighborhood of North Philadelphia East also saw a fall in income recently, dropping from $32,000 in 1991 to $28,000 in 2005–2006. In addition, home values are among the lowest in the city, with the median value placed at $18,400.

For most parents here, there are also choices to be made, but these decisions revolve not around the best preschool to pick, but the best way to provide food, shelter, clothing, and health care. These challenges remain constant throughout the child's entire life, due in part to the bleak job prospects for their parents. Unemployment runs high—nearly 29%, with little relief in sight. Less than half of the adults here have finished high school and fewer than 3% have attained a bachelor's degree.

A mother here—and over 75% of the children live in single-parent households—has few options for child care. There's the Head Start and Even Start federal programs, which offer high-quality but limited hours of care. More than likely, a child here will go to a local church-based program or be raised by a relative, such as a grandmother. The unsettling work patterns and varying shift schedules makes stability in child care nearly impossible.

Upon reaching elementary school age, the child from the Badlands is likely to attend one of the eight local public schools. Against all odds, these elementary schools have been highly successful, recording scores in math and reading above the norm. For a short period in one place—the elementary school classroom—children here stand for a brief moment on equal footing with their peers in Chestnut Hill. But one only has to look at the playgrounds at these schools to see how the immediate environment changes these children's future. Early mornings, principals and teachers pick up empty drug vials, hoping to shield their students from the realities of their neighborhood. Although by no means inevitable, starting around 7th grade, reading and math scores begin to fall precipitously. By high school, once-promising students start dropping out of school. William Penn, the local high school, has been slated to close for years, cited as one of the poorest performing schools in the city, with only 8% of students testing as proficient in reading and 12% in math. Thomas Edison High School does slightly better, with 25% of the remaining students scoring proficient in reading and 22% proficient in math. In 2010, 45% of the African American students graduated from high school; the rate was 49% for Hispanic students.

After-school programs are limited in the area, often staffed by inexperienced, undertrained volunteers. One or two decrepit playgrounds offer children a place to play. A few community organizations proudly exist, but their focus is on keeping the impinging ills that accompany poverty—joblessness, drug use, teen pregnancy—in check, rather than providing an enriching environment for children. Summers find children in local church-based camps, again with few resources, or worse yet, with nothing to do.

And so the students turn to the streets. Perhaps no consequence of such concentrated poverty is as destructive as the proliferation of crime and violence. According to statistics by Douglas Massey and his colleagues (Massey, Gross, & Shibuya, 1994), for every 1% increase in a neighborhood poverty rate, the major crime rate increases by 0.8%. As Elijah Anderson (1999) describes, it leads to the emergence of "the code of the streets," in which aggressiveness becomes a way of protecting oneself from the growing threat of victimization. Developing a threatening demeanor or cultivating a reputation for the use of force can be viewed as necessary adaptive behavior in a social world characterized by endemic violence. Ultimately, of course, it produces a self-perpetuating upward spiral of violence. Witness the startling statistics here: from 2010–2011, the Badlands had 1,714 aggravated assaults and robberies; Chestnut Hill had four.

EACH NEIGHBORHOOD, WITHIN THE SAME CITY AND WITH SIMILAR BEGINNINGS, has followed an entirely different trajectory. One has continued to thrive, while the other seems to have lost its way. These contrasting ecologies of affluence and poverty have become the source of increasing racial prejudice, growing class stratification, and widely different opportunities to become well-educated. As class tensions rise, urban areas like Philadelphia, especially in times of recession, experience escalating crime and violence. The poor become more disenfranchised and alienated while the affluent continue to build higher and higher walls to protect themselves from the rising tide of social disorder.

These "walls"—although transparent—have not gone unnoticed. To break them down, a number of major foundations in the city have focused their funding on creating comprehensive community-based initiatives, rooted in the belief that institutions can serve as key leverage points for stimulating social change. One such initiative came from the William Penn Foundation. Starting in 1996, the foundation launched a $20 million effort to transform 32 neighborhood branch libraries in the city into a technologically modern urban library system. Their goal was to enhance access to print and technology for all children and families in Philadelphia. Implicit in their efforts, though, was a wish to support diversity, cultural pride, and cultural pluralism as well as to further a sense of community throughout the "city of neighborhoods" in Philadelphia.

The idea of comprehensive community development is not new. Its roots lie in the settlement houses of the late 19th century and can be traced throughout the 20th century in a number of neighborhood-based initiatives, including the fight against juvenile delinquency in the 1950s, the War on Poverty in the 1960s, and the community development corporation movement of the last 30 years (Connell, Kubisch, Schorr, & Weiss, 1995). While varied, all of these initiatives have the goal of promoting positive change in individual, family, and community circumstances in disadvantaged neighborhoods by improving physical, economic, and social conditions.

For the William Penn Foundation, it was a bold and innovative strategy that rested not on the social pathology of economically distressed neighborhoods but on the capacities, skills, and assets of the families themselves in these neighborhoods. They recognized that even in the poorest neighborhoods, there are individuals, organizations, and resources that can help connect families, multiply their power and effectiveness, and begin to harness their energies for regenerating community. One place was particularly well-suited for this role: the neighborhood library. Committed to social justice and free and equal access for all, the library has been one of the few institutions that have historically focused on breaking down social, economic, and educational barriers.

The foundation recognized that libraries often serve as the heart and hub of many neighborhoods. Programs as varied as chess clubs, adult literacy, job services, immigration information sessions, and Internet training among many others offer a range of activities for children and adults, as well as meeting spaces for community activities. On an average day, in these often small, storefront libraries, you'll find groups gathering to socialize, to read the daily papers, and to enjoy the sense of belonging as if the library were a secular church or club. It sometime seems like the equivalent of the grown-up local hangout.

More importantly, these libraries also provide information, a critical pathway for social and economic mobility. And it was here, in particular, that the foundation sought some answers. It wanted to understand how the computerization of information might impact these communities. Would greater access to print and information break down some of the conventional walls that impeded educational attainment and social and economic mobility? Could libraries serve as a fulcrum for leveling the playing field? Might they serve to promote reading and the development of information capital?

We were asked to examine these and other questions in an evaluation of the change process. Taking a theory-based approach to our analysis, we focused on both the explicit and implicit theories of change that appeared to underlie the initiative. In theory-based evaluations, measures are developed

Chestnut Hill Library

that provide useful feedback to track the unfolding of these assumptions, to examine the extent to which the theory holds. Such strategies might include documenting progress, measuring inputs, holding focus groups, and examining a variety of contextual indicators. In the absence of a comparison or control group, an evaluator often establishes a counterfactual, comparing communities to assess how the experiences might differ among groups. The goal is to provide a textured picture of what is happening in a community and its implications for understanding human behavior, and for further research and broad policy directions.

From this framework, our study of Chestnut Hill and the Badlands emerged. Although in close proximity, these two neighborhoods represented exemplars of the new age of extremes: concentrated affluence and concentrated poverty. In each community, stunning Carnegie libraries–Chestnut Hill's in Georgian Revival style and the Badlands' Lillian Marrero in white limestone Grecian-style–both representative of their benefactor's largesse, stood as their center. From this vantage point we could study how each of these communities engaged students in the development of reading and information capital in a context where resources were fairly equal.

**Lillian
Marrero
Library**

ANY POLICY OR INITIATIVE must be based on a theory of action—a causal connection between the roots of the problem and the course toward solution. Ours is rooted in an environmental opportunity perspective (Neuman & Roskos, 1993). This view maintains that experience is one of the most important antecedents, if not the most important, for developing knowledge. Therefore, different opportunities for word and world knowledge—including access to print; level of exposure to written materials; and the amount of interest, attention, and communicative adult interaction provided to children early on—will set in motion a process that will either accelerate or delay the learning of skills related to reading and knowledge acquisition.

The consequences of these early experiences are enormous. It starts with the Matthew Effect, outlined in the now-classic studies by Keith Stanovich (1986), and his colleagues Herb Walberg and Shio-Ling Tsai (1983). Taken from the biblical passage that describes a rich-get-richer and poor-get-poorer phenomenon, this means that very early on in the reading process, poor readers who experience greater difficulty in breaking the spelling-to-sound code begin to be exposed to much less text than their more-skilled peers. Further exacerbating the problem is the fact that less-skilled workers will often find themselves engaged with materials that are either too difficult for them to read or too easy for them to learn from. This combination of difficulties in decoding, lack of practice, and inappropriate materials results in unrewarding early reading experiences that lead to less involvement in reading-related activities. Lack of exposure and practice delays the development of automaticity and speed in reading. Slow-capacity draining word recognition processes require cognitive resources that should be allocated to comprehension.

However, the disparity in reading experiences of students with varying skills extends beyond the immediate task of comprehension. Rather, it has consequences for their future reading, cognition, and the development of information capital. Stanovich and his colleagues (Stanovich, West, & Harrison, 1995), in subsequent research have found that the sheer amount of reading accounted for a sizable portion of variance in measures of general knowledge, even after general ability was partialed out. For example, in a study of 4th graders, Cunningham and Stanovich (1991) found that individual differences in word and world knowledge were predicted by exposure to print after controlling for age, memory, and nonverbal intelligence. Similar results were reported by Stanovich and Cunningham (1993) with undergraduate students as well. In other words, these studies indicate that the very act of reading can enhance the development of knowledge and verbal intelligence.

Consequently, the role of reading in the process of knowledge acquisition led us to propose the knowledge gap hypothesis (Neuman & Celano, 2006). If we assume that knowledge produces more knowledge, those who read more will engage more in higher-level conversations, learn more, and use information for fulfilling specific purposes and needs. Greater use enhances speed of information acquisition, leading to rapid, extensive, and automatic processing indicative of the first and most common mode of information capital. The intellectually disciplined process of actively and skillfully conceptualizing, applying, and/or evaluating information gathered from multiple texts in new digital environments support the second mode of information capital. Over time, with differential access, it is likely to accelerate a knowledge gap for those who have these opportunities and experiences and those who do not. And these differences may account for the social stratification of information capital that occurs among those who live in affluent and poor communities.

Therefore, the William Penn Foundation's effort to transform libraries into digital environments that could equalize resources in these neighborhoods where resources were hardly equal was especially intriguing to us. Although these libraries might represent only a small microcosm of their worlds, we could examine how "leveling the play field" in these environments might impact children's developing skills when they are learning to read and when they are reading to learn, developing the critical reading skills that will enable them to acquire knowledge and information capital.

IN EVALUATING THE INITIATIVE, the foundation's question was more straightforward: By equalizing resources across these disparate neighborhoods, might the knowledge gap between economically advantaged children and economically disadvantaged children in these communities close? Although we recognized the necessity of evaluating comprehensive community-based initiatives and the potential lessons to be learned and applied to the next generation of policies, programs, and resources, such initiatives have been especially challenging to researchers. It is about observing knowledge and practice, and not in an isolated laboratory setting, because literacy is so tied and firmly rooted in the community. For example, in a special report to the National Academies of Sciences, a study group concluded that although prevailing research methods may promote randomized control trials as the "nectar of the gods" (p. 12), alternative approaches are needed when you examine a community-based initiative (Connell et al., 1995).

In order to adopt such an approach, we spent thousands of hours in the neighborhood libraries. Basing our work on the environmental opportunity perspective, we focused on how the environment might influence behavior. We developed a series of studies to examine how these environments influenced individual behaviors and, in turn, how individuals influenced the environment, recognizing the reciprocal tensions that change both settings and individuals over time. Along with a multiracial team of ten doctoral students in urban ethnography from Temple University, we engaged in multiple field work techniques—situated listening, observations, interviewing. Examining environment typologically as a nested arrangement of structures and systems of interactions in the tradition of the brilliant ecologist Urie Bronfenbrenner (1979), we conducted studies that looked at the broader context of activities, such as access to resources in neighborhoods, to the context of the library through detailed ethnographies involving frozen time-checks to determine hour-by-hour involvement in the libraries and shadowings of personnel in libraries, to the specific interactions within the library with family, peers, the computer, and reading materials. Each study was informed by the previous analyses, giving us a richly detailed understanding of activities and interactions not limited to a single setting, but designed to contrast settings. In all, we conducted 21 different studies, the details of which are described in the Appendix. Here, however, we attempt to interweave our data to better understand how children from these two very different communities develop and become educated.

Our intention was to study these activities in the libraries throughout all phases of the 5-year community-based initiative. Instead, we stayed for more than 10 years. In the first years, our studies indicated a gradual but clear transformation from public libraries as book-centered environments to information- and community-centered environments, embracing multiple technologies and books. Trends in the computerization of information, transforming reading patterns and uses of knowledge, started forming toward the end of the first 5 years; it became increasingly important over the following 5 years to document how these patterns profoundly influenced reading and knowledge acquisition for students in both communities. In doing so, we attempted to describe how the geographic contours of concentrated affluence and poverty not only affected children's early years but also later development, when their identities and educational aspirations are forming. In essence, it is a portrait of how stratification works to maintain the status quo for some, and to undermine the educational opportunity for others.

CHAPTER 2

On the Streets Where They Live

Social stratification involves a set of calculations. It first divides people into categories based on a combination of achieved and ascribed characteristics such as income, level of education, prestige, or social standing; then it orders them in a vertical social structure characterized by a distinct top and bottom. Children reared at the top of the ladder typically thrive; those reared at the bottom do not, with patterns of underachievement especially stark for children of diverse cultural, linguistic, and racial backgrounds. Factors including low-income households, single parentage, limited education, and speaking a language other than English essentially add up to large estimations of risk for school failure.

Nevertheless, such definitions of social stratification hardly capture the complex dimensions of the social and economic environment, or the extent to which the communities in which these individuals live affect how they may fare. Consider, for example, the social isolation of a neighborhood like the Badlands, where corporate decisions have left emptied warehouses for blocks in a row, and where finding fresh groceries at a decent price becomes an arduous chore. Contrast this environment with the abundance of services, resources, and information that the more privileged communities like Chestnut Hill can easily access, and how this might affect behavior.

Consequently, differences in individual family status characteristics may actually belie a far more complex network of social class differences: People absorb from their immediate physical and social universe values and beliefs that guide their actions. It might reflect beliefs and actions about how to educate children, or loyalty to the local football team or commitment to a particular club or social action group. These environmental factors are not merely backdrops for understanding how children learn and develop in these communities. Rather, they serve as contributing factors for explaining differences in how people are likely to interact, behave, and ultimately develop expectations for achievement.

Geographic and spatial boundaries of neighborhoods, therefore, may exacerbate inequality by stratifying groups, not just individuals. A social environment's *affordances* or opportunities can affect what type of activities are likely to be available, the task demands, the mode of behavior, the purposes or motives of the individual participants. These settings come to shape children's cultural expectations about learning, literacy development, and what they may believe is achievable. It is here, in these day-to-day activities, where young children will observe and participate in the purposes and styles of interaction that are so crucial to their development.

From our perspective, then, we needed to understand how the physical and social environment might influence how children come to know and experience print in its many forms outside the library walls, before we could adequately gauge what went on within them. Although there has a been a plethora of research on the differences in socioeconomic status characteristics (e.g., professional occupations, income) in communities of affluence and poverty, differences in the environmental opportunities for engagement in print have been rare. Our strategy, along with our urban ethnography team, therefore, was to examine the amount and type of print resources and opportunities for children in each community. Throughout our investigation, we asked: How might the physical and social environment influence children who grow up here? How might it encourage or constrain certain behaviors? Given the importance of these early years, how might this environment contribute to children's growing understanding of print and its purposes?

With these intentions, we canvassed each neighborhood by walking the streets, riding the buses, and taking the subways. We visited community institutions in the neighborhoods, including child-care centers, elementary schools, and local organizations. Knowing that children learn about print through contact, experiences, and observations of written language used in their everyday lives, we looked at a range of experiences, trying to understand how the environment might either support or deny children's access to print. To better compare and contrast these environmental factors, we counted the print signs, labels, and logos; the quantity and selection of children's books that parents could conceivably purchase in the neighborhood; the public areas where children might observe people reading; the quantity and quality of books in the local child-care centers that children would most likely attend; and the quantity and quality of books in the local elementary school libraries. Although each of these influences most likely plays some role, together they play a powerful role in helping to shape young children's entry into print and the world of information.

Our process was like an audit as we examined the amount and quality of print that is essential to information capital formation in these two communities. And throughout these contrasts and comparisons, the message came through loud and clear: As you will see in this chapter, the streets where children live are categorically unequal in educational opportunity.

THE DISPARITY BEGINS with a common fixture in all neighborhoods: street signs. At first glance, it may seem inconceivable that something as ordinary as a street or store sign might influence a child's life. Nevertheless, studies suggest that children begin to define their world through signs and other print in their environment. Studies by Yetta Goodman (1984), for example, have shown that the quality of signs, their color, shape, and definitional scripts (e.g., "Hi! I'm Tony the Tiger") can be an enabler for young children, allowing them to practice what it is like to be a reader before actually being able to read. You'll find children identifying the McDonald's sign, or picking out their favorite cereal in the grocery store based on a Cocoa Puffs logo. Although they're probably not actually reading at an early age, children learn a wealth of information from these visually distinct signs. Product labels, restaurant signs, and street signs start to help them understand their environment, become involved in it, and remember this information for future occasions.

Walking through these neighborhoods, our research assistants recorded the name of every sign, its condition (e.g., good/identifiable or poor), and whether or not it provided a picture logo (e.g., like the McDonald's sign). We then totaled up our numbers and created corresponding percentages for each neighborhood and took photographs to illustrate the types and quality of the signs.

Table 2.1 describes the number and conditions of signs in the center of each neighborhood. Signs were more prolific in the Badlands, reflecting a larger census tract than in Chestnut Hill. However, the percentage of logographic signs and the condition of those signs differed strikingly from one another.

In Chestnut Hill, a 3-year-old would likely find a sign with an iconic symbol in good readable condition, professionally designed, with clear colors and strong graphics. Children could conceivably read their environment through these signs with pictures, shapes, and colors denoting the library, the bank, and the public telephone. Symbols like a bakery featuring a large *B* combined with a loaf of bread might even help a child connect the letters with their names, while also providing clear signals to what lies in store in these buildings.

Signs in the Badlands were more plentiful but of mixed quality; 74% were judged to be in poor condition while 26% were in good condition (see Figure 2.1). Many were covered with graffiti with taggers' distinctive

Table 2.1. Number and Conditions of Signs in Each Neighborhood

Neighborhood	Business signs	Logos	% Good condition	% Poor condition
Badlands	209	42	26	74
Chestnut Hill	77	28	99	1

Figure 2.1. Condition of Signs in Chestnut Hill and the Philadelphia Badlands

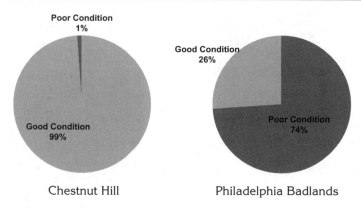

| | Chestnut Hill | Philadelphia Badlands |

signatures, rendering them impossible for a young child to decipher. Many of the poor signs were in total disrepair, such as a "Discount Food" store sign that is missing an *S*. Lacking funds for professional signage, business owners resorted to hand-lettering their own signs, resulting in faded letters and poor graphics. Street signs were often missing. Even the eagle on the U.S. Post Office truck was disfigured by graffiti, making the once-proud symbol nearly unrecognizable.

Signs are often children's first entries into print. They are markers, helping them to decipher their immediate environment. But even more importantly, they serve as a reflection of how a community views print. In Chestnut Hill, children will learn to understand a good deal of the purposes and processes of reading, of connecting print with meaningful activity just by strolling down their local streets. In the Badlands, such opportunities will be far more limited and narrow in scope. Here, signs are often inaccessible to children who might pretend to read them.

THE DIFFERENCES GROW DEEPER when we began to survey the number of print resources that might be available for parents and young children to read. We walked each block throughout each neighborhood, stopping at every store (e.g., bookstore, grocery store, bodega), likely to have reading resources for purchase: newspapers, magazines, children's books, and teen and adult books. We counted the number of titles, the descriptions of the types of materials, and age distribution. To the degree possible, we also counted newspaper boxes, newsstands, kiosks, and honor boxes.

Table 2.2 describes the number of stores in each area that carried children's books and magazines. In Chestnut Hill, 11 places sold print materials for children, seven of which even had special sections just for children. In

Signs in Chestnut Hill

Signs in the Philadelphia Badlands

contrast, the Badlands, which has a far greater density of children, had only four places that carried children's print materials. There were no bookstores.

Looking more closely in each area, Tables 2.3 and 2.4 describe an even more disturbing picture and equation. To examine the amount of choice a parent might have to select a book for a child, we counted the number of *different* children's titles in each store. Detailing the type of store, number of children's titles, and general type of reading material (e.g., magazines, books, comics), we found massive differences not only in number but in type of materials available. Children in Chestnut Hill, for example, had access to literally thousands of book, magazine, and comic book titles, whereas children in the Badlands had a small fraction of materials, less than 2% of their Chestnut Hill counterparts. There were about 13 titles for every 1 child in Chestnut Hill; whereas there was 1 title for about every 20 children in the Badlands. Most of the titles we found, moreover, were coloring books.

In the Badlands, parents of young children would find it difficult, if not impossible, to purchase a book of any quality in local stores; in Chestnut Hill, it would be hard to escape them.

Table 2.2. Number of Places Selling Reading Resources

Stores	Badlands	Chestnut Hill
Children's Resources		
Bookstores	0	3
Drugstores	2	2
Grocery stores	0	1
Bargain stores	1	0
Corner stores	1	0
Other stores	0	1
Children's stores	0	4
Total	4	11
Young Adult Resources		
Bookstores	0	1
Drugstores	0	0
Grocery stores	0	0
Bargain stores	0	0
Corner stores	0	0
Other stores	0	0
Total	0	1

Table 2.3. Reading Resources in the Philadelphia Badlands (Child Population: over 7,000)

Store name	Type of store	Children's titles	Young adult titles	Type of print resource
Rite Aid	Drugstore	112	0	Book/magazines (pictures, puzzle, comics, activity)
Rite Aid	Drugstore	142	0	Book/magazines (pictures, puzzle, comics, activity)
Chico's Cut Rate	Bargain store	95	0	Magazines (comics)
Maria's Candy	Corner store	9	0	Magazines (comics, puzzles)
Total		358	0	

IF YOU EVER WANT TO EXAMINE the density of print in a community, try the local barber shop. You might find old magazines, newspapers, and partially filled-out crossword puzzles—activities to keep you busy while you wait to get served. Or you might check out the local diner, laundromat, bus stop, nail salon, or any other place where you might have to kill time, and search for print. Now take in the other features of the place: whether there's comfortable seating, lighting, temperature, and the climate of the place, and see if you feel comfortable hanging out and reading there for a while. This is what we did to better understand how much an average child might learn about the forms and functions of reading by observing its daily use.

Children are great imitators. They begin to uncover the mysteries of written language by observing others and participating in literacy activities. From these and other demonstrations they begin to imitate some of the actions associated with reading and writing and become motivated to learn more about it. We reasoned, therefore, that regular, routine, and habitual uses of reading in public might support the view that reading is important, enjoyable, and pervasive in a community.

To examine reading in public places, we asked our research assistants, now quite familiar with the community, where one might be able to get a cup of coffee and a newspaper and sit for a spell and relax. We eliminated any outdoor spaces like parks, since winter was quickly approaching. Residents were asked to identify at least five places in each neighborhood. These included laundromats, bookstores, pizza parlors, bus stops, diners, coffee shops, hair salons, and fast-food restaurants.

In these establishments, we focused on what was being read, by whom, and for how long. We also examined environmental features of the setting, the lights, and seating, and how they seemed to support or detract from

Table 2.4. Reading Resources in Chestnut Hill (Child Population: 1,200)

Store name	Type of store	Children's titles	Young adult titles	Type of print resource
Borders*	Bookstore	14,000	Unspecified	Book
Christian Literature Crusade	Bookstore	640	0	Books (toddler, picture, coloring)
Philadelphia Print Shop	Bookstore	1	0	Books (coloring)
CVS	Drugstore	7	0	Books (coloring)
Eckerd	Drugstore	34	0	Books (toddler, workbooks, coloring/ activity)
Superfresh	Grocery store	6	0	Books/magazines
Chris's Store	Children's store	10	0	Unspecified
Benders	Children's store	1,000	0	Unspecified
O'Doodles	Children's store	115	0	Books (toddler, picture, educational coloring, family style art)
Mes Enfants	Toy store	120	0	Books (toddler, picture)
Performing Arts Store	Other	520	0	Books (scripts, scores, toddler, stories, multicultural, dance, biography)
Total		16,453	0	

*Shortly after our counts, Borders Bookstore in Chestnut Hill closed, cutting the number of children's titles by about 85%.

reading activities. For example, without much lighting in a coffee shop, it would be nearly impossible to read more than a few words without strain. In fact, we ended up looking for the presence or absence of 17 features in these establishments across the neighborhoods. These included such factors as comfortable seating, lighting, temperature, attitude of the proprietor, and ambiance of the setting. Table 2.5 describes the environmental features that related to whether the setting was convivial to reading.

In raw counts, as you'll see in Table 2.6, once again, there were large discrepancies: In Chestnut Hill, 82% of establishments provided the resources, comfort, and ambience that seemed to support reading; in the Badlands, 47% were conducive to reading.

Table 2.5. Environmental Factors Influencing Public Places (Spaces) for Reading

Factor	Description
Available seating	With the possible exception of bus stops, people need seating to read for any sustained period.
Comfortable seating	The level of comfort of seating seemed a deliberate choice by the proprietors, depending on whether they wanted patrons to remain at the establishment for a long time.
Availability of reading materials	In the majority of cases, reading occurred when there were reading materials within the immediate vicinity (i.e., newspaper boxes, newsstands, bookstores, used papers).
Presence of other readers	Other people present engaged in reading
Tolerant management	Although not economically desirable for them, managers who would allow and encourage sitting without purchasing for periods of time supported reading.
Comfortable temperature	Places where the temperature (air-conditioning or heat) was controlled supported sustained reading, in contrast to places (like a laundromat) that were hot and stuffy.
Seasonal weather	Outdoor weather influenced whether people would read outside or not.
Adequate lighting	Some level of lighting was required to read anything.
Nondisruptive noise level	Soft music and quiet conversations supported reading, in contrast to places with, for example, very loud music or screaming children.
Nondisruptive activity level	Places that were relatively serene with minimum distraction were more conducive to reading compared with areas where there was hustle and bustle.
Lack of competing activities	Other time-killing activities did not compete with reading (e.g., video games, television).
Presence of corroborating activities	People seemed to read in places where they could concurrently eat, drink, and/or smoke.
Good ambience	The atmosphere seemed to invite reading activity (e.g., Borders).
Friendly staff	Waitstaff encouraged hanging around, often knowing patrons by their first names.
Plenty of surrounding space	Some level of privacy (e.g., empty chairs, tables) seemed to provide a sense that spending time reading was appropriate.
Cleanliness	Areas that were relatively clean supported reading, in contrast to places that were dirty and trash-ridden.
Aesthetically pleasing	Establishments pleasant to the senses—sight, smell, sound, touch, and taste—seemed to influence hanging out and sustained reading.

Table 2.6. Evidence of Environmental Features in Places (Spaces) for Reading in Public

Stores	Badlands	Chestnut Hill
Available seating	2	5
Comfortable seating	1	3
Availability of reading materials	1	5
Presence of other readers	2	3
Tolerant management	2	3
Comfortable temperature	2	4
Seasonal weather	5	5
Adequate lighting	5	5
Nondisruptive noise level	4	3
Nondisruptive activity level	3	4
Lack of competing activities	3	4
Presence of corroborating activities	2	4
Good ambience	0	4
Friendly staff	0	3
Plenty of surrounding space	2	5
Cleanliness	3	5
Aesthetically pleasing	3	5
Total percentage of places	*47%*	*82%*

But in this case our counts did not convey the differences we found. For example, let's take two restaurant establishments, one in each of the neighborhoods. Just down Germantown Avenue in Chestnut Hill, there's a popular place to sit for a spell, the Trolley Car Diner, located at a busy intersection. As customers enter, they can grab a newspaper or magazine at one of the three news boxes located directly outside the restaurant. Much like a typical diner, inside this establishment there are ten booths, a few smaller tables, as well as padded stools. The stereo is tuned to an oldies station.

The mood is comfortable and friendly. Waitresses convey a maternal manner, calling customers "hon" and chatting informally with some. The restaurant has its regulars who are eating a late lunch. Two customers are reading newspapers and are nursing cups of coffee for over an hour. Several used newspapers are folded on a counter next to the coat rack for anybody who wants them. Each waitress takes orders, brings food, and then intrudes only when someone nods for a check or a coffee refill. With the presence of people reading and sitting for long periods of time, little hustle and bustle, and print resources in close proximity, the place seems pretty conducive to reading activity.

Contrast this scene with places in the Badlands. Here there are only a few fast-food places and delis, and even fewer sit-down restaurants. For folks wanting to sit and eat, the only option might be the local Popeye's Chicken and Biscuits. The place seats fewer people than the Trolley Car's; Popeye's booths are hard, and the lighting is fluorescent and overly bright. Although there is only one person eating at the restaurant at the time, this does not suggest that business is slow. On the contrary, business is bustling and brisk. Orders are to take out, and booths are mostly for temporary waiting. At one point, three men play video games, killing time until their order is ready, but leave soon after they get their food. The proprietor and employees seem to encourage the quick turnover, looking at hangers-on (us, for example) suspiciously. Others come in, sit at the booth, and eat but do not linger. There are no reading materials available either in or outside the restaurant and we see no reading activity of any kind.

This pattern we describe would repeat itself many times in the other settings we visited. Overall, the public places in the Badlands were not conducive to reading. Seating was uncomfortable, not sufficient for the number of people who would regularly visit or wait; lighting was often glaring; and business owners were more often than not intolerant of hanging around if there was minimal or no financial gain. There were no reading materials, and no corroborating activity. Contrary to the sit-down and linger activity in Chestnut Hill, there was a take-out and to-go pattern of activity in the Badlands.

The reasons that these examples are important are that children learn about the importance of literacy from observing its use in daily practice. They often model what they see. In Chestnut Hill, they will likely observe the sheer prevalence of reading in all aspects of daily activities. They will see people using reading while eating, relaxing, waiting, and doing errands. Lacking conducive environmental supports in public settings, children from the Badlands would likely observe reading in private spaces or perhaps on the run.

PRESCHOOLS AND ELEMENTARY SCHOOLS are often seen as the safety net for children who may come from low-income communities. Nevertheless, the pattern of wide disparity between our neighborhoods persists even in these settings. We examined book access in the local preschools, hoping to find book-rich settings that would compensate for the lack of print options in the neighborhood. Rather than count the number of books, here we were interested in the quality of the book selection. We used an adaptation of a common environmental quality measure known as the *Early Childhood*

Figure 2.2. Quality of Books in Local Preschools in the Badlands and Chestnut Hill

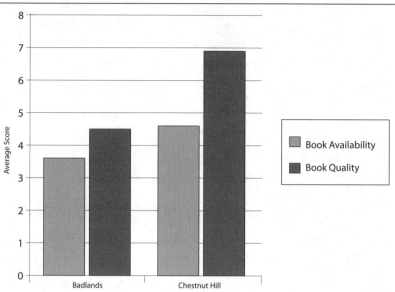

Environment Rating Scale (ECERS). Generally a minimum criterion score of 5 in each category is used to indicate good quality, with a range of 1 (poor) to 7 (excellent) possible in each category.

Upon visiting 20 preschools, ten in each neighborhood, we found a predictable pattern. Book collections in Chestnut Hill, predictably, were close to excellent (6.9). These centers included attractive displays of books, a variety of genres so that children could be introduced to poetry, information books, classics, and folktales. Book collections in the Badlands (4.5), on the other hand, were adequate (see Figure 2.2). Selection was limited but the books were in pretty good condition. Largely subsidized by state funding, budgets for books were in a general supply category; center directors often had to use these funds for basic supplies. Given the increasing number of children who spend the greater portion of their day in child care, differential access to resources appears to add yet another factor to the equation of inequality.

STILL ON THE HUNT for that precious safety net, we visited the local elementary school libraries. Given that the district of Philadelphia funds all public school libraries, we expected parity here. You would naturally expect schools in one area of the city to get the same amount of funding as in the other—perhaps even more if funds from Title I, the federal elementary and secondary act targeted to low-income children, were applied.

Example of a Classroom Library in the Philadelphia Badlands

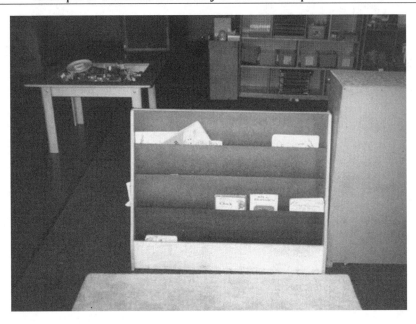

Limited Print Exposure in Classroom in Philadelphia Badlands

But this was not the case. In fact, our analysis of school libraries indicated a sharper pattern of inequity than what we had previously seen in the schools. We concentrated on three categories of access: resources (including number and condition of available books and computers), staffing (e.g,. librarian's training and years of work experience), and availability (e.g., the number of days the library was open per week).

Throughout the Badlands, the school libraries were in serious disrepair. As shown in Table 2.7, the number of books per child averaged 12.9 for the Badlands; books ranged from poor to good condition. By contrast, there were 25.7 books per child in Chestnut Hill. For every computer in the library in the Badlands schools, there were three in Chestnut Hill. Staffing also varied considerably. There were no trained school librarians available to children in the Badlands, whereas school librarians had master's degrees and an average of 12 years of school experience in Chestnut Hill. Staffing issues, of course, affected the number of library hours or days the library was made available. On average, libraries were open about 3 days a week for children in the Badlands (ranging from permanently closed to 5 days a week), compared with 5 days a week in Chestnut Hill. Essentially, children who lived in already print-rich environments tended to have school libraries that offered more books, more computers for research, better trained librarians with more experience, and more hours to visit during the day. Unfortunately, those children likely to benefit most from school libraries were offered the poorest services, resources, and access on fewer days of the week.

THIS IS WHERE INEQUITY IN EDUCATIONAL OPPORTUNITY begins. Differences in the economic circumstances of children who live in these neighborhoods translated into extraordinary differences in the availability of print resources. At every level, we found inequities: in the number of

Table 2.7. Condition of School Libraries in Chestnut Hill and the Badlands

Area	Average number of books	Books per child	Condition of books	Average number of days open per week	Librarian (degree)	Average number of computers
Badlands	5,400	12.9	Poor to good	3.8	No trained librarian	1.4
Chestnut Hill	7,700	25.7	Good to excellent	5	Yes (MS or MLS)	4.0

resources, the choice and quality of materials available, public space and places for reading, and the amount and quality of literacy materials in child-care centers and in elementary schools.

Further, differences in access to print begin to cascade into another set of relationships that play a vital role in children's reading development. For example, Adriana Bus and her colleagues (Bus, Van Ijzendoorn, & Pellegrini, 1995) have estimated that the best predictor of early reading achievement is the amount of time parents spend reading to their children. The prevailing assumption, however, has been that books and other literacy related resources are easily and equally accessible to all children and their families. Our analysis challenges this assumption. It builds on a growing body of ecological research that examines access to literacy as a potential contributing factor for explaining differences in interactions, behaviors, and ultimately achievement for young children.

Social anthropologists (Cole, 1990; Scribner & Cole, 1973) have suggested that such differential access may support different types of cognitive routines. For example, children who have been read to frequently often internalize a story structure—an understanding of how stories work, demonstrating how basic mental processes and activities become integrated through experience (Stein & Glenn, 1979). In a community where print is ubiquitous, children are likely to develop certain assumptions about how written language works and will internalize these scripts, pretending with their friends that they are ordering from a restaurant menu, reading from the newspaper, or other literacy-related activities.

Moreover, since print is a primary source of information, early access to resources begins to build the important background knowledge that is essential for later understanding of reading materials. Early access to print enhances the speed of initial reading acquisition, setting in place the power to read widely in multiple genres. Limited access to print, therefore, may not only delay the initial reading acquisition process but the process of learning words, concepts, and knowledge that will be critical for understanding print and its purposes and potential uses.

Beyond the "picture perfect" setting of Chestnut Hill, then, lies a set of resources, physical and social, that are likely to help children get off to a good start. Young children growing up here will likely see an abundance of resources tied to information capital and print in their surroundings. They will observe people using print in their daily interactions, and begin to form an understanding of the multiple functions and pleasures of reading. In the more densely settled, isolated neighborhood of the Badlands, children will experience resource deprivation. There will be few print resources in close proximity to where they live and fewer opportunities to see it regularly modeled. This ecology of inequality may come to define those children who are prepared for the ways of learning and thinking that are nurtured in school, and others who may develop problem-solving skills that are either unacknowledged or run counter to school learning. For these children, it is the streets where they live, complicated by social, economic, and physical disparities, where educational inequality may first take root.

CHAPTER 3

The Paradox of the Level Playing Field

Although "stark" and "defining" may describe the differences in print resources throughout the neighborhoods of Chestnut Hill and the Badlands, enter the local libraries and you enter another world. Here, for all intents and purposes, resources are fairly equal. Book collections at both branches are extensive, with nonfiction sections full of local culture. You can find an old favorite or something brand new in the varied fiction collections, and borrow an eclectic assortment of music CDs, audiobooks, or DVDs. Branch managers are experts about their local communities, knowing many of their patrons by name. Children's librarians are welcoming, knowledgeable, and never seem to have met a child they couldn't wow with a good book.

In these stately stone buildings with their tall, arched windows and high ceilings, there's a natural experiment in the making—an ideal setting to watch how reading patterns compare in these two communities where the playing field of reading resources is more level. Although the Chestnut Hill branch might boast that it has 34,747 items in its adult/teen collection and 24,306 items in its children's collection, compared with 23,489 items for adults/teens and 17,953 items in the children's section at Badlands' Lillian Marrero branch, both create a similar effect (at least to the untrained eye). What you see is akin to a candy store of reading choices, including newspapers, magazines, and books on every imaginable topic.

In this chapter, we explore a central premise of our theory of action, one that underlies many policies and programs for low-income children and their families (e.g., Title I programs, Head Start): Namely, in a situation where resources are fairly equal, might the activities associated with them look similar for children and their families from very different socioeconomic circumstances? It allows us to examine the role of material resources in equalizing opportunity in reading and acquiring information. For example, if resources alone may account for differences in reading and information capital, then one would assume that by equalizing them we would see comparable patterns of reading across communities. However, if this is not the case, it might help to identify other factors that relate to our environmental opportunities perspective. In the second part of the chapter, we highlight these factors, examining how different parental and adult support systems may influence children's initial exposure to print.

Because reading patterns vary for adults and children, we examined general reading patterns for three age groups in both neighborhoods: adults, teens, and preschoolers. However, in this first analysis, we quickly learned that a library is more than a repository of books and materials. On a daily basis, you'll find people engaged in a wide variety of activities, such as reading, attending events and special projects, socializing with friends and neighbors, and checking out and returning materials. It can be challenging to examine how reading occurs in a library setting. Traditional approaches such as turnstile counts don't take into account the rationale for visits or the activities done within libraries. Further, you can't necessarily rely on circulation figures to examine reading patterns, since these numbers can be notoriously inaccurate for libraries in poorer communities because of their heavy dependence on library registration, cards, and fines.

Therefore, we developed a technique used throughout our study to closely examine patterns of reading and activity in the libraries. Mapping the activity settings broadly in each library, we focused our analysis first on adult reading activity, visiting each library for 20 hours, 2 hours at a time to represent all available hours. We then turned our attention to the young adult area, and finally to the preschool area. During each visit, two research assistants observed and recorded the individual who entered in the reading area, the type of reading resource (book, magazine, computer, or newspaper), and the average time spent with each reading item.

This is how we began to discover a fundamental paradox in reading patterns across these two communities: When the playing field is equal, striking similarities initially appear in the patterns of reading in these two different neighborhoods. It's not until you look below the surface that you find an equally striking pattern of differences, reflecting both the immediate effects of the environment and its longer-term impact on the development of information capital.

FIRST, LET'S TAKE A LOOK at the adult population. Most striking is the similarity of reading among adults across these two libraries. Each hour, our research assistants count about four new people who enter the adult area to read in Lillian Marrero; similarly, about four enter the area in Chestnut Hill. At Lillian Marrero, adults spend an average of 42 minutes reading; at Chestnut Hill, they spend an average of 41 minutes reading. In both communities, adults visit the library primarily for information. In fact, we calculate that about 99% of the reading resources selected are nonfiction, with much of the time spent reading newspapers and magazines, as well as reference

Figure 3.1. Mapping the Activity Settings in the Library

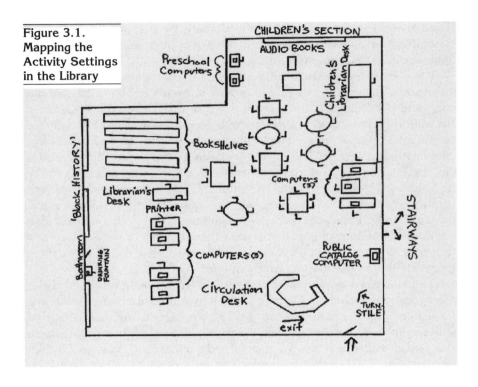

Table 3.1. Adult Activity in the Library: Chestnut Hill and Lillian Marrero

Characteristic	Chestnut Hill	Lillian Marrero
Total number of adult patrons	72	72
Median reading time (min.)	41	42
Gender	60% F 40% M	60% F 40% M
Ethnicity		
Caucasian	80%	–
African American	18%	65%
Latino	2%	35%
Reading Materials		
Nonfiction (reference, newspapers, magazines, etc.)	98%	96%
Fiction	2%	4%
Total number of hours observed	20 hours	20 hours

materials and nonfiction books. Only a small percentage of time is spent reading fiction by patrons at either library.

Now let's move to the young adult section. Here, the activity in both libraries is more dense and active. We tally 157 teenagers, or about 8 teens per hour, who spend time at the Lillian Marrero library, and 115, or about 6 per hour, who visit from Chestnut Hill. But this time we begin to notice a curious pattern. Despite the rich treasure trove of books, newspapers, and magazines available for these teens, we find that some of the students are reading books and materials designed for younger children. In other words, they read "down." For example, you might see a 13-year-old boy reading *Arthur's Eyes*, a book more appropriate for the elementary school crowd. We start recording the particular titles that students read in order to examine this phenomenon more systematically; specifically, whether the book might reflect at, below, or above the students' age-level reading.

We find that, in both libraries, the teens have a shorter attention span with reading than do the adults. The average amount of time is only about 10 minutes with multiple reading materials, suggesting that they spend about 3½ to 4½ minutes per reading resource. But here is where the similarities in reading patterns for these young teens end. When we calculate the amount of time spent reading "down" compared to reading at level, or even "up," reflecting challenging material for their age, we begin to see a troubling

Adult Activity at the Lillian Marrero Library

pattern for the students from the Badlands compared to Chestnut Hill. In the Badlands, although students read at their age level about 58% of the time, 42% of their time is spent reading down. You might see, for example, early teens reading *Highlights* magazines, books from the Dr. Seuss collection, even board books—materials that are far below their age level. Compare this with students from Chestnut Hill; in this case, most of the teens' reading is at their age level (93%), with a small percentage of reading "up" or more challenging above-level materials (7%).

Here, in essence, is the paradox: although the amount of time spent reading is almost equivalent in both settings, the challenge level is strikingly different. In one library, students seem to consciously select too-easy

Table 3.2. Teenager Reading Activity in Public Libraries

	Chestnut Hill	**Lillian Marrero**
Number of children visiting library	115	157
Gender	70% female 30% male	50% female 50% male
Average age of child	15 years old	15 years old
Accumulated minutes of reading time	1,153 minutes	1,523 minutes
Average reading time per child	10 minutes	9.7 minutes
Number of minutes per reading activity	4.5 minutes	3.6 minutes
Number of various reading materials per child	2.2	2.6

Table 3.3. An Example of Reading Activity in the Library: Lillian Marrero, 2:30–4:30 p.m.

Gender/ age	Reading activity	Time	Age level/ material (approximate)
1. Female/14	*Spot Goes to School*	2:59–3:00	Below level
	Wibbly Pig	3:01–3:02	Below level
	Where Does It Go?	3:03–3:05	Below level
	A Very Mice Joke Book	3:12–3:26	At level
2. Female/16	*Bill Cosby's The Day I Was Rich*	3:32–3:38	At level
3. Female/15	*Push, Pull, Empty Full* (board book)	3:40–3:43	Below level
	The Cheerios Counting Book	3:45–3:47	Below level

Figure 3.2. Level of Reading Material

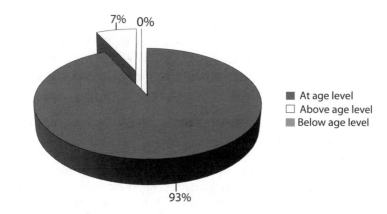

Children from Chestnut Hill neighborhood

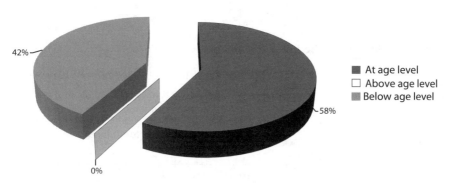

Children from the Badlands neighborhood

materials; in the other, students tend to seek to read at either their age or challenge level. Given that these low-level resources are likely to have limited relevance to their current lives, we wonder why would students from the Badlands on their own select materials of lesser challenge than others? Could it be because these students are poor readers, still learning to read when their counterparts are reading to learn? Does it have something to do with self-efficacy, their perceived beliefs about their reading abilities? Or might it reflect how they are socialized early on about reading and its purposes? We turn to our next activity pocket, the preschool setting, to look for the answers.

IN THE OFTEN-CAVERNED PRESCHOOL SETTINGS, we adjust our strategy to try to unravel this paradox. Instead of conducting timed analyses, here we looked at the activity pocket of the setting more globally to understand how children become socialized around books. We conduct our observations in 2-hour increments for a total of 20 hours in each setting, attempting to capture interactions with toddlers and preschoolers around books. Additionally, we note the approximate length of stay throughout the visit as well as the family member who generally accompanies the child.

And in contrast to all the common patterns we recorded before, our observations indicate stark and discernible differences–in attendance, activity, length of stay, number of check-outs. These differences reflect how children are socialized to engage with reading resources early on.

These patterns are described in Table 3.4. It all starts with the adults. In the Chestnut Hill library, for example, children always seem to enter the preschool area accompanied by an adult–most often their mother but it may occasionally be a father, a nanny, or a grandmother. In comparison, in the Badlands, young children almost always enter alone, sometimes with a sibling, but very rarely with an adult. With little to do, children wander in and wander out, with relatively little focus.

Table 3.4. Activity in the Preschool Setting of Libraries

	Chestnut Hill Library	**Lillian Marrero Library**
Attendance in library	Always accompanied by an adult/parent/caregiver	Rarely with adult; more likely alone, or with peer/sibling
Mentoring	Child given great deal of direction/scaffolding highly interactive	Little to no mentoring/direction
Book selection	Adult analyzes appropriateness of selections for children, guiding/directing choices	No guidance
Checkouts	Books always checked out	No check-outs
Length of stay	Relatively short but purposeful visits (about 20 minutes)	Long visits (sitting with others in other areas of library) Often frenetic, short bursts in preschool area
Computer use	Child and parent engaged in activity	Child alone or with older children If around, adult inactive
Librarian assistance	Not available	Not available

For children in Chestnut Hill, the activities are highly routinized. Invariably, the accompanying parent takes charge, suggesting books, videos, or audiobooks to check out. Sometimes the parent might pull a book down and let the child examine it or ask a child what types of books to look for. But the parent is clearly in charge: in a very authoritative manner, they sometimes note, "That book is too hard for you," "That is too easy," or "This one might be better." Parents steer children to challenging selections, sometimes appeasing them with a video selection as well. Visits are brief, highly focused, and without exception, end with checking out a slew of books, and often DVDs.

Children in the Badlands, on the other hand, receive little direction. Occasionally an older brother or cousin might help locate a book or read to them. But more often than not, we see short bursts of activity, almost frenetic in nature. With little direction, children will pick up a book far too difficult for them or much too easy. Although the average visit to the library is longer than those we see at Chestnut Hill, often the time is spent sitting with friends or siblings in other sections of the library. Rarely are books checked out.

These comparisons and contrasts, however, don't adequately convey what you are likely to see in each library. Rather, you have to observe the day-to-day activity to see what it looks like.

INSIDE THE SPACIOUS PRESCHOOL AREA at Lillian Marrero, separated from the rest of the library by "castle walls," you'll find bins and baskets, crates and shelves full of books and computers. On an average day, you will often see little kids–3 and 4 years old, some maybe even as young as 2–wander in. They are almost always alone.

There's a rather frenetic scene in this section of the library. Young children will come into the area, flip through some pages of a book, and leave. *Flipping* is a term we come to use to describe what a very young child will do without adult assistance. He or she will pick up a book, look at the cover, pause for a moment to try to figure it out, and then put it down. Flipping is a short-burst activity; typically, a child will spend no longer than 2 minutes before the frustration mounts.

Here are some examples. A boy, age 4, comes into the preschool area, takes a Richard Scarry board book from a basket, sits at a low table, and flips through its pages. This is a book with single words next to the pictures, and it seems to hold his interest for only a moment or two. He puts it down and picks up a Magic School Bus book. He flips through this, but it holds his interest for even less time. These books are complicated, with complex ideas and hard words, and are dense with print. He tries one more, hardly making it through even one page. He puts the book down and walks out.

In another case, a toddler walks in and looks through the basket of board books. She selects a book, tries to turn the pages, and looks at one of the pictures. She appears momentarily mesmerized by the picture, and turns to look for help. But no one is there; she drops the book and scoots out of the area.

Sometimes an older sibling accompanies a little brother or sister, and spends some time in the area. An 11-year-old accompanies her 4-year-old sister, selects an alphabet book and flips through it quickly, pointing out the letters as she reads. The preschooler becomes engaged, but the big sister finishes it as fast as she starts it, and both are out of the area within 2 minutes. About a half hour later, they come back to the area, and the big sister picks out another book. Now the little sister wants nothing to do with her, and moves to another child in a pink dress who is "reading" a book aloud. The big sister gets angry and yells, "Don't mess with me. Come sit down now!" But the little sister stays with the other little girl in the pink dress and they look at big books for about 3 minutes. All three girls then leave the area.

Occasionally, a parent will accompany a child in the area. We watch a father with two children in tow enter the preschool area. He spreads some papers on a table. "Go sit down! You're in a library!" he says in a loud whisper. "Go get a book," he orders. One child sits in the stroller while the preschooler picks *Henry's 100 Days of Kindergarten,* a brightly illustrated picture book and starts to page through it. After a few minutes, she turns to her dad and says, "Can you read this? Please?"

Looking like he'd much rather finish his work, he gives in. Sitting next to him in the little chair, he begins to read haltingly, pointing to each word as he goes. "In February, it sn . . . sn . . . um . . . snows." In June, Henry likes . . . ice . . . cream." He stops, "Hey, ice cream," recognizing the word he just decoded. "I love ice cream, don't you?" The little girl positively beams. He takes about 10 minutes to read the book, studying the pictures and saying each word slowly as he points. When he's finished, she asks, "Can I take this home?" "Not this time," he answers.

Other parents seem distracted, lost in their own world. A mother sits 10 feet away in a chair marking her book with a yellow highlighter while her 6-year-old son explores the stacks alone. He forays several times for books, returning with selections to show his mother for her approval. "No, we've already seen them," she says, sending him back to find something new. He returns several minutes later. Collecting what appears to be one, two, or three items from him, the mother gathers the rest of her belongings. Before she heads for the door, she points to the librarian who is now sitting at her desk. "Say bye to the lady," the mother says to the little boy. "Bye, bye, lady," he dutifully responds.

AS YOU ENTER THE PRESCHOOL AREA of the Chestnut Hill library, you are immediately confronted with a bit of a crowd scene—the couplings of parents and children together, poring over books, making selections, or just reading together. In quiet voices, you hear a good deal of "parentese" talk—the singsongy set of tones that the mothers and fathers use when they are talking with their young children. A mother will slow down her language, and articulate each sound as her child looks at the pictures in a book. In response to her 18-month-old toddler's interest in reading "Pip-Pip," the mother grabs the book *Pippa the Dinosaur* and says, "That's right, it's Pippa the Dinosaur."

The parents are highly attentive to their children. Phoebe, age 2, bounds up to her mother with a board book to read. Although her mother is talking to a friend, she stops and instantly turns her attention to her child. She reads the first page, "I've got sunshine on a cloudy day." As the child looks at the picture, her mother adds, "I think this is a song." She turns the page. Phoebe points to the baby in the photo and the mother asks her, "What is the baby doing? What does this baby have?" Little Phoebe doesn't answer. The mother asks another question, trying to help Phoebe respond. She points to the colorful toy guitar that the child in the picture is holding. "What is that?" No answer. "What does this look like?" The mother gently persists. Phoebe whispers in her ear, "A guitar." "Yes. It's a play guitar, but not like Daddy's. His is made of wood. Who is holding the baby?" Phoebe answers, "A daddy." "Yes, it looks like Daddy." The interaction comes as close as you can get to a textbook example of instructional scaffolding, the kinds of helpful interactions between adult and child that enable the child to go beyond his or her current expertise. The mother clearly defines her expectations, and at the same time, supports Phoebe's ability to negotiate meaning through oral language.

Parents' guidance and scaffolding go beyond the interactions with books. It's almost like a hands-on "how to" on the library. Parents authoritatively guide and select their children's reading choices. For example, a mom and her little girl about age 4 are picking out some books in the area. They do not stay long. "Oh, look, they have *Brown Bear!*" the mom tells the little girl, trying to steer her toward books in a basket on the floor. The girl, however, is more interested in the nearby rack of videos. "No tapes," the mom says. "You have so many tapes at home. Let's get some books." She picks up about 10 books, and they go to the checkout desk.

Here's another example. A mom heads over to the area with two children. "These are books on kittens and cats," she says to the girls. They sit down on a bench, and the mom starts reading but then realizes the text is really too difficult and boring for the girls. "Oh, look," the mom says, "this cat is having kittens. " The girls respond to the mom's questions. They close the book. Then one girl picks up another cat book (it looks very old and worn). Mom says gently, "No I think this one is better" (picking up a more recently published book). They grab the book and go to the checkout.

Many parents will tell you that the library is a weekly destination stop, often coordinated with the story-time hour given by the children's librarian. When we meet up with 2-year-old Alara's mom Anna Maria, she's quick to talk about her daughter's interest in books, despite the limitations of her daughter's patience and wandering ways. "Alara is not an easy toddler at story time," says Anna Maria. "Most children sit still and listen. Mine? She's more active. Sometimes I have to go running after her," as she shadows her daughter who, as if on cue, starts meandering.

In the course of Alara's wanderings, we see another aspect of this social environment in the library: groups of mothers and toddlers who meet weekly to socialize. Alara, in this case, meets up with three of her toddler friends. She opens up the book she's carrying and shows them a double-page spread, carefully holding it toward them like a storyteller. "What's her name?" asks a little blond boy pointing to the figure on the page. The children sit down around Alara. "Okay, Alara, tell them what's happening," prods her mother. As Alara looks down on the top of the paperback book, she begins to tell a story. One of the mothers quips, "It's 'pre-story time' story time."

It's difficult to distinguish Alara's toddler language, especially over the din of the growing crowd in the vestibule area, but that doesn't seem to bother the other children. They are enraptured. Listening on, Alara's mother suddenly bursts into laughter as she realizes that the story Alara is telling has nothing to do with the pictures in the book. Quietly to the other mothers, she says, "She's showing them a book about Snow White, but telling them about her favorite story, 'Little Mermaid'." The toddlers, however, seem oblivious to this distinction as she goes on with her story.

THE PARADOX OF LEVELING THE FIELD is that in equalizing resources, the field is still unequal. Material resources, even when they are comparable in libraries, represent only one kind of support in creating an environment for reading development. Rather, there is a more critical factor. For behind the seeming comparisons and contradictions and the "Tiger Mom" phenomenon and backlash, is the reality of the "affordances" of social class. Parents' active monitoring and guiding in their child's activities at Chestnut Hill are closely aligned with "concerted cultivation," the child-rearing strategy identified with middle- to upper-middle-class families by University of Pennsylvania sociologist Annette Lareau in her book *Unequal Childhood* (2003). These mothers often have the luxury of part-time employment and/or nannies which allow them to devote "quality time" to their children. In contrast, children in the Badlands are more likely to be raised in a spirit of "natural growth. " Many of these parents work many hours at low-paying jobs and struggle with ever-changing work shifts. As a result, young children often spend less time in the company of adults such as parents or teachers, and more time with other children in the kind of self-directed, open-ended play for which affluent parents often profess nostalgia these days. Nevertheless, the effects of these differing strategies—which are not only a matter of resources but also of beliefs and habits—are to reinforce class divisions. They help to prepare Chestnut Hill children for life in the middle and upper classes by accustoming them to ask (and nag and negotiate) for what they want. It ultimately infuses them with a sense of entitlement that comes from having so much of the family's life formatted around their activities. Natural-growth children, on the other hand, learn implicitly and explicitly through observation and their own experiences.

In this context of early literacy, these differences have profound implications. In the spirit of concerted cultivation, toddlers and preschoolers in Chestnut Hill appear to be carefully mentored in selecting challenging materials; in contrast, those who experience the process of natural growth in the Badlands receive little if any coaching. Left on their own, these children resort to playful activity of short bursts, picking books up and putting them down with little discrimination and involvement. In Chestnut Hill, activities are carefully orchestrated to encourage reading for individual growth and development; in the Badlands, no such mentoring is available—they are on their own.

We returned to our mechanism of counting participation in the area in 2-hour increments to examine how these patterns may potentially influence early reading development. As we did before, we count the age of the child, whether he or she is accompanied by an adult, and the content of what they read. We note, in particular, the amount of text the child is likely to encounter in a visit.

The patterns are clear. In Chestnut Hill, for every hour, 47 minutes—more than three-quarters of the time—is spent by an adult reading to a child. Estimating the number of words children would hear within this hour (e.g., based on the length of the book, and the time spent reading) we calculate about 2,435 words and their referents in print. During the same time period, not one adult entered the preschool area in the Badlands. A generous estimate of words likely experienced in the 1-minute flips is 180 words, none of which are "read" to the child or decoded. By our estimate, we figured that children in Chestnut Hill hear nearly 14 times the number of words in print than those in Lillian Marrero.

PERHAPS NO OTHER TOPIC in early childhood has been as well researched as the shared book-reading experience (National Early Literacy Panel, 2008). Parent-child book readings are associated with children's overall reading readiness, their understanding of print conventions, and vocabulary (Mol, Bus, deJong, & Smeets, 2008). Studies (Cunningham & Stanovich,

Table 3.5. An Average Hour of Reading Activity in the Library

Gender/age	Reading Activity	Time	# of pages/ words read	Companion/ relationship	Companion Reading Action	Time
Chestnut Hill Library						
Male/6	Arthur's Computer Disaster	3:15–3:19	10/330	alone		
	Berenstain Bears (BB)	3:20–3:26	all/100	C, f, 30/mother	read to son	3:26–3:39
	SpongeBob Stop Presses	3:26–3:39	all/1000			
Male /6	Curious George	3:36–3:40	all/500	alone		
Female/2	Bug Your Mom	3:40–3:44	all/300		read to girl	3:40–3:44
	Daddy's Little Girl	3:44–3:46	all/300	C, f, 25/caregiver		3:44–3:46
	Berenstain Bears (BB)	3:46–3:48	all/100			3:46–3:48
	Baby on the Way	3:50–3:55	all/1,000			3:50–3:55
Male/6	Superheroes	3:55–4:15	20/1,240	AA, m, 30	read to self, listens to son reading	3:55–4:15
Totals:		60 minutes	4,870 words			47 minutes
Lillian Marrero Library						
Male/5	My Favorite Dinosaur	10:50–10:51	5/40	alone		
	Curious George	10:51–10:52	3/24			
	Happy Easter Maisy	10:52–10:53	3/24			
Male/5	My Favorite Dinosaur	10:54–10:55	4/32	alone		
	Happy Easter Maisy	10:55–10:56	3/24			
	Curious George	11:09–11:10	5/40			
Female/4	My Favorite Dinosaur	10:55–10:56	6/48	alone		
	Happy Easter Maisy	10:56–10:57	4/32			
	Red Train	11:12–11:13	3/96			
Totals:		9 minutes	360 words			0 minutes

1998) have shown that even simple stories for 2- and 3-year-olds like the *Curious George* series include complex words and phrases with a much higher incidence than in daily communication. When these favorite stories are repeated again and again, like we see with Alara and her friends, children develop deeper vocabulary and understanding of print concepts.

Still, high-quality parent-child interaction around books provides an even richer experience. For example, a recent meta-analysis extracting data from 16 eligible studies showed the added value of an interactive shared book experience as opposed to passive participation by the child (Mol et al., 2008). When parents approach storybook reading deliberately, using strategies to encourage the child to talk about pictured materials and providing informative feedback by expanding, corrective modeling, and other forms sensitive to the child's developing abilities, the book-reading experience is further enhanced.

Less recognized about shared book reading, however, is the amount of information that is acquired through these parent-child interactions. Exploring the maternal input during storybook reading, University of Michigan psychologist Susan Gelman and her colleagues (Gelman, Coley, Rosengren, Hartman, & Pappas, 1998) have shown how parents go beyond simple word labeling routines by providing a rich array of information. In their conversations, parents stress, in subtle and indirect ways, concepts that help children categorize information. They also generalize category information using generic noun phrases that enable young children both to organize information efficiently and to extend knowledge beyond what is already known.

As a facet of conceptual development, categorical membership has a unique potential as a self-teaching device; that is, once a category has been learned, a child may use information about a category to generalize to new instances. For example, when presented with a novel word like *katydid* and told it is an insect, a young child can infer properties about a katydid based on his or her knowledge of other insects. Studies (Neuman & Dwyer, 2011; Neuman, Newman, & Dwyer, 2011) have shown that very young children can use category membership to extend knowledge and specifically to make novel extensions.

In other words, there is a bidirectional relationship between word learning and conceptual development (Kaefer & Neuman, 2011). For example, we engaged 109 Head Start children in a small-scale test using a match-to-sorting task. An experimenter pointed to a target item (e.g., tarantula) and asked the child to "choose the one that is the same type as this item." The potential match items consisted of a category member (e.g., grasshopper), something that was thematically associated with the item (e.g., honey), and a distracter item (e.g., shoe). We found that the proportion of words that children learned predicted greater categorical sorting and that more categorical sorting predicted the proportion of new words children were able to identify. Namely, word learning supports children's conceptual organization, which facilitates new word learning.

Words, then, are not just words; they are signifiers for interrelated bundles of knowledge. The reason we need to know the meanings of words is that they point to the knowledge from which we are to construct, interpret, and reflect on meaning in oral and printed text. They are the interface between communication and thought.

So let us return to our paradox, and try to understand the connections between these preschool years and the later years, when teens are reading on their own. In the earliest years, middle-class parents like those in Chestnut Hill endeavor to teach children the words that they will need to know through rich experiences with books. They do not do this intentionally but implicitly by reading many different texts. Many of the stories they read will include words that recur over and over again, as well as many, many words that will arise only infrequently. With each new book, therefore, children will be provided with a basic review of common words and an introduction to new words. In essence, each book will bootstrap the language and knowledge needed for the next, gradually enabling the child to be ready for texts of greater complexity and depth. As the young readers' linguistic and conceptual knowledge grows in richness and complexity, it will increasingly support their ability to predict new words in context, infer the meanings of many new words, and the representation of many new spheres of knowledge.

Now in the case of young children in the Badlands, even in the best of circumstances, the words they will encounter in these brief flips with books are likely to be made up of relatively few words that recur over and over again. For example, in the three pages of written text in *Curious George*, a child will likely encounter 14 lines of print, or 96 words. All of these words are common, with the exception of the now more-uncommon term "straw hat," which is also illustrated on the page. If the book was read to the child, it would likely increase his or her understanding not just of the common words that were in the text but the uncommon ones as well. However, as you see in the Table 3.5, the 1-minute flippers go from book to book, never accumulating either the common words or the more unusual ones. Without the adult to scaffold their learning, it is highly unlikely that children would accumulate any word knowledge.

What this means is that children from Chestnut Hill are likely to start off with not only a richer vocabulary, as numerous studies have documented, but a self-learning mechanism that will allow them to effectively and independently use the context of varied texts to acquire more knowledge. Those in the Badlands will need to rely on school instruction, which if provided, can significantly increase their knowledge of words. However, as cognitive scientist Marilyn Adams has calculated (Adams, 2010), even if beginning in grade 1 and continuing through grade 12, teachers consistently taught and students perfectly retained 20 words each and every week, the gain in vocabulary would only total 8,640 words in all (20 words x 36 weeks of school x 12 years), ten times less than what is required in high school. Further, as they are acquiring these words, they will be missing the knowledge networks that evolve and become more sophisticated through reading.

Consequently, students' intentional selection of less challenging texts may not only result from the lack of modeling and guidance provided early on by the parent. It may be that these children early on have been denied the very language, information, and modes of thought they need most to move up and on. Flipping books in the early years is a poor substitute for being read to. It indicates children's eagerness to learn, but it also indicates their lack of access to print without the scaffolding support of the adult. By the time they get to be teens, they may be reading easy texts, like the patterns we report in the Badlands, and not acquiring the words, concepts, and mode of reasoning that will be essential for building, modifying, and refining knowledge. In contrast to their age level, their vocabulary level and conceptual development may be at these lower-level texts.

PARENTS, HOWEVER, ARE NOT the only educators in children's young lives. Other active social agents in children's immediate environment play an important role in early learning. As psychologist Urie Bronfenbrenner recognized in his ecological systems theory (1979), early schooling and the neighborhood in which children live will have a coercive influence. And it is here where the contrasting ecologies of affluence and poverty seem especially stark for children who live in such concentrated neighborhoods.

It occurs early on, when children are toddlers and preschoolers. As poverty or privilege concentrates, knowledge of what one does to prepare children for school pervades, extending beyond the parent-child relationship to preschools and programs in the local neighborhood. You can see it in the way children are encouraged or discouraged to ask questions, to engage and construct new understandings about books and print, and to freely converse with adults other than their parents.

WE ARRIVE IN THE CHESTNUT HILL LIBRARY close to 11:00 a.m. when the weekly half-hour story time for toddlers is about to begin. The room is packed with 30 parents and 45 children, the two back doors virtually gridlocked with strollers.

Today Kate Bowman-Johnston, the 20ish bright-eyed, effervescent children's librarian, has planned for a busy program. She opens with a poem sung to a familiar children's tune: "Good morning to you, good morning to you. We're all in our places with bright shining faces." With the children now situated and focused, she segues into a more active song, telling the children that "when you hear the color that you are wearing stand up and clap your hands," and begins singing to the tune, "If You're Happy and You Know it." "If you're wearing red today, please stand up." Next come directions for children wearing "green," then for others wearing "stripes." Nearby 2-year-old Valerie sits cuddled in her mother's arms and points to a woman on the side of the room who is bouncing a 6-month-old baby. "She has stripes," Valerie says, tugging at her mother for attention. "Yes, she has stripes," her mother affirms. Bowman-Johnston finally concludes the song with directions for people wearing "any color today."

She begins another song, "You put your right arm in, you take your right arm out. You do the hokey pokey and you turn yourself about" and goes on to directives for "left arm" and the "head." The latter stymies a 2-year-old who can't seem to figure out what to do with her head. Gently from behind, her mother shows her how to put her head in. The child then does it alone.

Today, the storybook *Tanka Tanka Skunk*, by Steve Webb, is about an elephant and a skunk who love to do rhythm and rhyme and greet other animals by pounding out the syllables of their names on drums. "Now we'll be clapping along to this book," says Bowman-Johnston. Many of the parents are holding children in their cross-legged laps, modeling by clapping their hands against their children's legs—one clap to beat the cadence of each syllable of the rhythm. "Ti-ger, chee-tah, pan-da, pol-ar bear," repeat the mothers and children.

As the book progresses, the text moves from simple to more challenging meter and even tongue twisters.

"Cat-er-pil-lar, big gor-ill-a, yak-et-ty, yak-et-y, yak."

"Pan-da, pan-ther, tig-er, ze-bra, all-i-ga-tor, fox."

Now Bowman-Johnston ups the ante. Beginning in a high-pitched whisper—"Tin-y, lit-tle, hair-y spi-der"—she alternately lowers her pitch and escalates her volume as she reads through the rest of the words on that line: "arm-a-dil-lo" and ultimately, "ox." The parents and the children follow her prompt, pretending to use their whisper voices when going to bed, and loud voices when waking up again.

As the half-hour program comes to a close, parents and children sing a good-bye song, pick up their carpet squares, and place them in a stack. Parents gather and chat with one another, offering hellos to many of the children around them or asking about lunch plans. Clearly, there is a sense of community among them.

It's like this every Tuesday. About 75–80 people show up each week to hear the librarian engage toddlers in vocabulary games, syllabic rhythm and rhyme, along with the fun and motivating world of storybooks. Bowman-Johnston would like to cut down the numbers, finding it all a bit unwieldy, but the mob scene at the checkout desk offers evidence that she can't. With some 6–10 books cuddled in their arms, these young toddlers are in for a busy week of reading.

IT'S DIFFICULT TO COMPARE THIS SCENE to one you might see at the Lillian Marrero library. Not that the branch doesn't dutifully conduct a story hour, which it does. Rather, it's the people that attend the story hour. At the Lillian Marrero branch, nearly all the children who come to the story hour are from the local day care centers out for their weekly group excursions.

As we enter the storybook area, it's not exactly bedlam but precipitously close. The 32 children seem to roam everywhere, grabbing books and throwing them down. With much shushing and outright yelling, the providers finally get them seated. Some children pick up books from the bins or shelves and are looking at them. Four boys crowd on the floor around a book called *Spiders.* "Look, six eyes!" one them cries, and they all count the spider's eyes.

The lead provider is clearly annoyed. Her assistant tries to help, but their collective patience has worn thin. "Can't we read?" whines one little girl. "Sitting here is getting boring." "Put those books away" yells the provider. "Who says you could read? We're playing the Quiet Game." "Everyone, put things away and get on the rug!"

The group finally settles, and Sara Palmer, the children's librarian, takes her seat on a small stool in the front of the room. Her presence seems to do in 3 seconds what the providers tried to do for 15 minutes. She starts reading *Slop Goes Soup,* a book with great sound effects. She reads with great verbal and nonverbal expressions: "Slop!" "Slither" "Crash!" "What do you think is going to happen?" she asks at one point. "He's going to crash!" they chime joyously.

Sara reads: "Giggle, giggle. Boys and girls, can you giggle?" she asks, and they giggle heartily. And on a page where a character is sneezing: "Ah-ah-ah-ah!" "Choo," the children call back. She finishes the book and takes out another, this one titled *This Is the Rain.* "Where does the rain come from?" she asks. "The clouds! The sky!" they say in unison.

Meanwhile the lead provider in the back of the room is looking on, completely indifferent. Her assistant is checking her cell phone. One of the aides is filing her nails while the other has gone to do an errand.

Completely enthralled by Sara's readings, however, the children are distracted from this scene, too busy learning about the ocean, clouds, and rain and the worlds these words conjure up. After she finishes, they groan a little bit and say their good-byes. Dashing to the door, it's back to bedlam. There is not a parent to be seen.

TO OUR OBSERVERS, these scenes crystallize a pattern of behaviors that reflect disparate philosophies and provisions for education in these two communities. As affluence grows more concentrated, so too does a certain ethos about children's education. It is no longer enough to ensure that their children receive all the benefits that are possible to be successful; clearly, there are high hopes of making their children their little prodigies. Competition for education becomes ever more fierce. Parents not only nurture their children; they compete amongst themselves to ensure that children read the "best" books, receive the "best" child care and go on to attend the "best" schools. Even in the library, parents orchestrate their activities, socializing with others who they regard as well-educated and successful. By the time these children reach their teens, they are independent readers, ready to read and engage in challenging topics and texts.

As poverty grows more concentrated, the "hands-off" approach to education reaches beyond the parents to early schooling, where children's interests are stymied by disinterested teachers who themselves may be beset by multiple difficulties stemming from a lack of income. The numerous demands on parents' time as they grapple with the manifold problems due to their own lack of income make the supervision and monitoring of children's activities nearly impossible. These children are given nurturance but of a different kind. They are encouraged to be independent, and in the process of making their own way, they learn important life skills. But the skills they do not receive are those essential for early reading development. For these skills, there is no replacement for the guidance and scaffolding from an adult.

THE ANSWER TO OUR PARADOX lies in a scene we see at the Chestnut Hill library after a long day. A woman in her 70s with silvery gray hair is sitting at a table reading *What Spot?* to a 2-year-old girl who is sucking her thumb and wiggling in the chair next to hers. The book choice is rather surprising; it's an "early reader" book—one with minimal artwork to illustrate the rather Spartan vocabulary and simple sentence construction intended for older children learning how to read on their own.

Still, with their heads scarcely a foot apart, the woman leans down toward the child pausing after every one of the brief sentences. She looks into her eyes for emphasis. Slowly, the child moves closer to her grandmother. As she reads, the child turns away from the book to study her grandmother's face. With her right hand, she rubs her grandmother's earlobe. The grandmother continues reading without pause. Then the child gently shifts her tiny body around so that she is again facing the book, stuffing her left thumb in her mouth, while at the same time never letting go of her grandmother's earlobe with her other hand. Her grandmother's gentle intonation continues, pausing at times for effect until they finish the lengthy story. Not wanting to intrude, we leave, wishing only that we could have seen this same scenario across the miles-wide divide at Lillian Marrero.

CHAPTER 4

The New Work, The New Play

The transformation of the libraries into modern technology centers in Philadelphia began in the late 1990s. There had been a clunky computer or two in the adult or teen section, and up until this point, most of the libraries had only limited technology resources. Now in a dazzling display of renovation, gleaming banks of new computers complete with cutting-edge software and Internet access stood at the very center of each library, along with well-defined preschool areas boasting the latest in computer technology for the younger set. Working with neighborhood groups, architects added a "wow" factor to encourage nontraditional patrons to the libraries, creating distinctive designs and murals to reflect each branch's local culture, heritage, and talents, and children's librarians and technology specialists were there to give any neophyte a helping hand.

For residents of the Badlands, the arrival of technology represented nothing less than the ultimate expression of hope for leveling the playing field. For decades here, the digital divide had loomed large. Despite technology's ubiquity in homes throughout Chestnut Hill, you would rarely find an adult who owned a *working* computer, and it would be even rarer for that person to have Internet service anywhere in the Badlands neighborhood. In fact, at the time of renovations in the late 1990s, less than 30% of their children under 6 had ever used a computer compared to 75% of their counterparts from Chestnut Hill.

The new technologies and their supports, therefore, were particularly welcomed in neighborhoods like the Badlands. Local efforts—coordinated by long-time librarian and resident activist Lillian Marrero, the library's namesake—even added $25,000 to the building fund to continually update the equipment. The excitement was palpable.

For our team, it raised a series of important questions: As a primary information source, would this new technology provide the early exposure to print essential for reading development, putting children like those in the Badlands in a better position to start reading early? Given the wizardry of these machines and their ability to support children's self-teaching, might we begin to see a closing of the opportunity gap? And would our traditional views of reading from print media dramatically transform to newer forms of literacy?

In this chapter, we first go back before we go forward. We first look at the reading landscape in each of the libraries before technology was ever introduced. Then we take a look at activities several years later, after the novelty of the technology is gone. We do this for two reasons. First, this analysis will give readers a better understanding of the significance of the William Penn Foundation's initiative to transform library environments into technology centers, especially for children and their families in low-income neighborhoods. Second, it provides an important context for the patterns we are about to see in computer use among young children and their parents in our two neighborhoods.

Next, we examine the promise of these digital resources early on in the process, when children are just beginning to develop the speech-to-sound code. According to our theory of action, if these digital tools could provide greater exposure to print, and potentially bootstrap children's early experiences with the alphabetic system, then we might be able to contain the Matthew Effect by ensuring that children could develop the sound structure of spoken words highly predictive of reading success. Unlike reading materials, computer programs have the capacity to take on some of the roles of the authoritative parent. With just a flick of a switch, mastery learning, problem solving, and the world of information are now at children's disposal, with verbal and visual prompts that place even 3- and 4-year-olds in control. Ten years ago, it would have all seemed unimaginable to think that very young children could build their cognitive capacities at their own pace. Now, we examine whether these capabilities can possibly contain the Matthew Effect.

WE HAD A UNIQUE OPPORTUNITY. As part of our analysis of the community-based initiative, we had carefully recorded reading activities prior to the introduction of technology in these libraries. As the technology opened up new possibilities for communication and information, we were then able to compare how reading habits evolved in these communities. In this respect, we were able to examine the potential transformation of reading as well as its potential displacement in favor of other activities.

Using an ethnographic technique we called frozen time checks, we observed libraries for every hour they were open during one solid week during this late 1990s research phase. Like a freeze-frame, once an hour we would take stock of where people were in the building and what they were doing. For example, we counted the number of people reading, hanging out, or checking out and returning books, and calculated an average percentage of the total time spent on a particular activity. We conducted these frozen time checks in two distinct periods: once before much technology was evident (e.g., two old machines that had been dedicated to teenage homework activities); and then, 5 and 6 years later after the technology was in place and the novelty had worn off.

Here you will see the percentage of people involved in activities over an average week in each library. As Figure 4.1 shows, activities in a neighborhood library are typically more varied that most people think. Although reading activity is always present, a good number of people are engaged in other activities, such as special projects, programs, short-term activities like photocopying, or just simply hanging out. Take a look at activities *prior to* technology in the libraries and you will find a very different pattern of activities in these two libraries. Even though the technology was poor at the time, a certain number of patrons in each community spent time on those old computers. However, in Chestnut Hill, most of the activities were related to reading, browsing, and checking out books. In the Badlands, on the other

Figure 4.1. Chestnut Hill and Philadelphia Badlands—Before Technology Changes

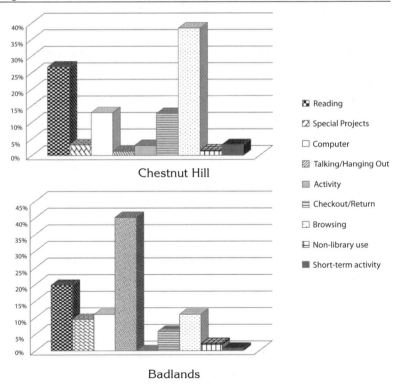

hand, not much reading was taking place; rather, the favorite activity was talking with friends and hanging out. It was a safe place to be.

Just 6 years later, as shown in Figure 4.2, we see a dramatically different picture of activities, particularly for the patrons in the Badlands. Looking across the landscape of activities, the central activity has become using the computer. Students may be hanging out, but they're hanging out around the computer. Time spent with books from time 1 to time 2 has significantly declined. Strictly isolating book and computer activities in Figure 4.3, the patterns become even more distinct. In the Badlands, computers seem to have displaced books. In Chestnut Hill, however, no such reversal has taken place; rather, here people have stayed glued to the books.

This pattern, of course, may be related to access. For families with limited access to these resources in the home, the library has become an important safety net. For families in homes where computer access is ubiquitous, such as in Chestnut Hill, no such safety net is needed. What the data do show,

Figure 4.2. Chestnut Hill and Philadelphia Badlands—After Technology Changes

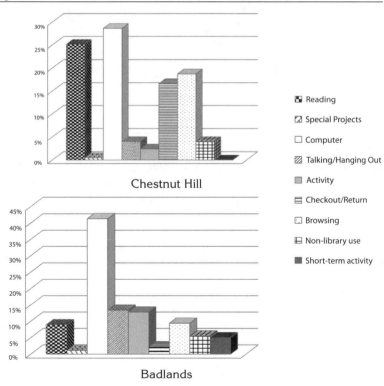

Figure 4.3. Books and Computer Use Before and After Technology

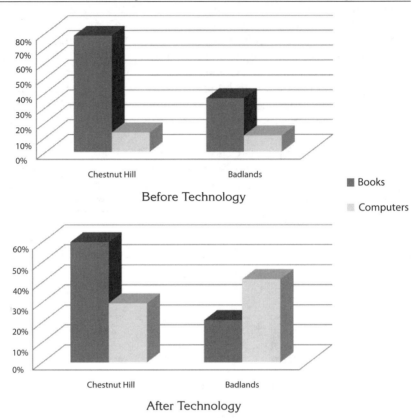

however, is that in these immediate contexts, the digital divide is somewhat alleviated. Consequently, it gave us an opportunity to ask: How might technology work to close the gap? Given its virtual capacities to travel the information highway regardless of where you live, might technology break down barriers to access and build information capital? To address these questions, we start in the beginning, where information gathering starts—when children are first learning to read.

THEY CALL IT THE "SIMPLE VIEW," but it is hardly simple. It is the process of learning to read. Coined some 20 years ago by reading researchers Philip Gough and William Tunmer (1986), it goes like this: If a child is both rapid and fluent at decoding unfamiliar words and can understand spoken language, you can safely predict that he or she will be a proficient reader. But the other side of the coin also holds true. If a child has deficits in either decoding or language comprehension or both, then it's safe to bet that there will be problems. You can't read if you can't decode and you can't understand if the words represent gibberish. It's a simple equation: R (reading) = D (decoding) x C (comprehension).

The simple view, in other words, is actually pretty complicated. It is hard work to learn to read. The availability of computers, however, is changing the nature of this work. With their flashy capabilities, computers can draw children in to work that looks like play. At their most very basic use, computers can make the first part of the reading equation—the learning of letters and sounds—seem easy. Basic decoding skills—figuring out what those inexplicable letters say—can be tackled through game-like formats that make the old drill and practice a thing of the past. In dazzling displays, computers can drill children in letters, sounds, and basic phonics. They can make kids practice for as long as they may need to reach automaticity. With the newest software geared to individual children's skills, computers can adapt strategies to help students develop mastery. They can monitor children's progress. As a relentless teacher, the computer can demand perfection in performance. And it can do all of this efficiently.

This process of learning to read is what we set out to examine starting from about 2002, after the initial novelty phase was over, through 2007. Our purpose was to explore the capabilities of these computers to level the

Young Child at Computer

playing field, getting children off to a good start at the very beginning of the reading process. For us, it was relatively new ground–to study how toddlers and preschoolers might use these wondrous machines for learning. Unlike book reading, at least initially, we could not anticipate the particular "rules of engagement" around the computer; the types of interactions, the kinds of playful conversations, nonverbal behaviors, and silences that might occur in these settings. Therefore, in these first years, we watched, wrote many notes, and then returned with these weekly observations to discuss them with our research team. In the later years, we returned to our process of counting, examining the time spent on activities, and the activities of the adults who might accompany the child.

What emerged in our analyses, at first, might seem counterintuitive. It counters much of what we expect in closing the digital divide. For in contrast to bringing the worlds of these young children in these neighborhoods of concentrated affluence and concentrated poverty closer together, computer technology seems to be drawing them worlds apart.

WITH ITS SMALL-SCALE FURNITURE and its sense of detachment from the rest of the library, the early learning computer station at the Lillian Marrero library is a bit of a haven for the younger set–toddlers and pre-schoolers, and their siblings and friends. The computers are standard issue but the keyboards are child-friendly, brightly coded with primary colors to identify the alphabet keys apart from the function keys. On the monitors, icons of a musical keyboard cue children to a host of math and reading choic-es and other programs. There's the Curious George software featuring a nice reader-friendly voice, the Reader-Rabbit learning to read series, the Kidspi-ration software, and book-game sets like *Stellaluna, Cat in the Hat, Green Eggs and Ham,* all seeking children's attention.

The play, however, is not as self-sufficient as it appears. Toddlers and preschoolers, although they appear capable, are not all that intuitive at ne-gotiating the software. Subtle things throughout programs require adult as-sistance and interpretation. This occurs with both the nomenclature, such as a "mouse," a term that doesn't make sense to a small child, as well as the poor choice of words sometimes chosen to illustrate the lessons, including the letters of the alphabet.

Without help, children can revert to random clicking–similar to the "flip-ping" we recorded with books. Alone, for example, we watch as a preschooler runs her cursor over a few icons, each which shouts out its name. Picking one called Green Eggs and Ham, she clicks on it and two options appear: "read to me" or "play the game." She starts the game, but can't follow the narrator's directions. Soon she clicks to another program, eventually becoming equally frustrated. She starts clicking away randomly, switching from program to program. In less than 2 minutes, she clicks, switches, clicks, switches about 20 times. As her frustration grows, she starts pounding on the keys as if they are a piano—that is, until the computer screen freezes and shuts down.

She needs help, yet behind her, sitting quietly, is her mother who is watching. She does not offer assistance. There is no interaction between them. Once the program freezes, the child runs off in another direction with her mother trailing behind her.

This is the pattern we would come to document after the technology had been in place for about 2 years. With little supervision, random clicks would inevitably lead to computer freezes, breakdowns, and frustrations. We reasoned, however, that once the adults became more comfortable with computers, and once the technology glitches could be sorted out, patterns would change. And we were right—to a degree. The technology did improve, with computers less susceptible to freezing and breaking down. But the patterns of the adults in these settings remained remarkably stable. In the Lillian Marrero library, children were generally on their own.

In 2006, for example, we observe a mom and her four tots, about 3 and 4 years old, all watching the *Green Eggs and Ham* story in the computer area. The children are glued to the screen. It is very much like TV—the words come up on the screen and a narrator tells the story accompanied by sounds and music. The group watches it for about 10 minutes. The mother sits toward the back of the group. She says nothing, and there is no interaction or discussion about the computer activity at all. After the program is over, one of the children pulls up a reading game associated with the story. This game requires the group to become more involved. One child controls the mouse ball; the others are really lost about what to do. "How do you do this?" one boy asks the mom. She shakes her head and does not offer help. The boy clicks away, obviously lost. Soon an older girl, around 12 years old, comes over and takes control. She takes over the activity as the other children watch. After a few minutes, the mom gets up. "Come on, it's time to go."

Sometimes, we observe parents trying to cheer on their children—but from afar. We watch a small gang of little boys, ages 4 through 9, playing a game. We quickly see that the 5-year-old is clearly in charge. The older child tries to take over but has to ask the 5-year-old what to do. Together they play for at least 20 minutes. At various times, the mother calls out encouraging things, such as "Way to go!" and "How about that!" Other than that, she does not comment. She stays in the background the entire time. Children address their questions to the 5-year-old, who "knows more than any of us," said the mother.

Parents' discomfort with these machines is often palpable. One mother, for example, tries to start one of the programs for her young toddler. After one try, she gives up, asking an assistant to "find her something to do with alphabets." With a bit of time on his hands, the assistant tries to explain the procedure: "You've got to close one program, click on another to get into JumpStart Toddler, and here's the activities to do with the alphabet." The mother moves to a nearby table, demonstrating through her body language that she wants nothing to do with any of this. Her daughter ends up using Green Eggs and Ham, wildly guessing the letter and word combinations. Occasionally, she gets it right, and is rewarded with an audio outburst or a visual reward such as fireworks, and some distant clapping from her mother. Never does her mother say a word.

At times, it almost seems like cyberphobia. We watch two children, ages 5 and 2½ enter the preschool area with their grandmother. Instantly, the 5-year-old boy bolts to one computer, while the toddler runs to the other, yelling "Me, me, me!" as she tries to climb up on the chair. "No, you are too young!" the grandmother says. After a bit, the grandmother relents, and asks a librarian if her 2½–year-old can use the computer. "Sure," the library aide replies, "but you will need to sit with her." "No!" the grandmother answers. "I don't know a thing about computers!" She turns to the little girl says, "The librarian says you are too young!"

Just then, the 5-year-old calls to his grandmother, "Can you help me?" he asks. Very reluctantly, she walks over and eyes the monitor and keyboard. "Well . . . it . . . it looks like you just need to type your name." Together, the grandmother and her 5-year-old grandson scan the keyboard and slowly hunt and peck for each individual letter of his name: D-A-V-I-D. He eventually plays the game—alone.

Computers can seem like a baffling blend of complication and mysticism to an adult who has not grown up with them. It might be nothing more than an electronic machine that can do all sorts of calculations and retrieve information with incredible speed, but to the uninitiated, it can appear superhuman. For adults who have limited experience with computers, interactions with the machine may seem to express something about themselves, their competencies—who they are as well as who they are not. Especially in front of their children, they may feel vulnerable and unmasked in their presence.

This vulnerability is often made clear by how the parent physically positions himself or herself, which defines the activities in the preschool computer area at Lillian Marrero. Instead of sitting next to their toddlers or preschoolers, they sit behind them, or in a different section of the library. Rarely do we see any discussion, interaction, or comments throughout the children's activity. Rather, it seems like the computer is in charge, not the parents.

Without parental support, the computer begins to take on a role we had not anticipated in our initial analysis: that of the video arcade. Despite the carefully crafted phonics lessons, alphabet activities, and well-told stories, most software programs reward children by playing games. Just like the video arcade, children can move through lessons rather haphazardly—selecting options at random to reach the ultimate reward: fireworks, clanging of bells, and/or shoot 'em-up galleries. Left to fend for themselves, this is exactly the activity we found young toddlers and preschoolers engaged in on the computers at Lillian Marrero.

AMBIVALANCE might be the best word to describe parents' reactions to the preschool computers at the Chestnut Hill library, at least when they first arrived. Frequently parents would steer children away from them, saying, "We're not here for the computers. We're really here for the books!" But especially in the beginning when children gravitated to the computers anyway, mothers would remain highly involved in the process. Rather than fight it, they soon joined in on these activities.

From the child's perspective, however, you might say that using computers in the library comes with a cost. For their parents, computers are not playthings; they are important teaching tools. You can see it in their posture at the computer. In contrast to the positioning of parents at Lillian Marrero, here the parent often sits close to the screen and leans forward.

Four-year-old Scott and his mother are having a great time playing Millie's Math House. He is using the mouse and generally doing okay. His mother gives him directions, encouragement, and suggestions on how to play. She is very involved, laughing when something amusing happens on the screen and rubbing his back when he does something right. She is seated very close to him and very close to the screen. "See that one has seven jellybeans, but you need five jellybeans for it to go into the number-five slot. So what do you need to do?" Scott clicks on the appropriate thing and his mother rubs his back, saying "Good job!" He stays with this activity for a while—about 10 minutes—while his mother continues to sit with him.

Although borrowing books might be the focus of these parent visits, the computers are the children's. Responding to children's interests, parents will put their books aside to assist them. One mother, already with a pile of picture books, runs after her toddler Ava who sees Reader Rabbit Toddler on the computer screen. Immediately it becomes a teaching lesson. "Okay, Ava, you need to match the *J* to the *J* train. That's right, '*D* is for *door*!' Okay, you have the *D* now get the *E* and where's the *F*? There you go!" Since Ava appears to have the hang of it, the mother goes over to browse more picture books. She's gone only a few minutes when Ava starts to flounder. "Mommy," she calls, "I can't do this!" With a little sigh, the mother pulls herself away from the books and sits down again. She starts to play the game, talking as she goes. "See, this is the letter *Y* and this goes there. And here's the letter *N*." She plays a few more minutes, with Ava watching intently. "Now, let's check out these books."

Children as young as 2-year-old like Ava are introduced to letters and sounds with the help of their parents in these playful formats. There's 3-year-old Lucas gazing at the screen where an animated train pulls across the screen with three cars in tow, each with a letter of the alphabet emblazoned on its side. Below the row of railcars on screen are a row of three large skeleton keys of similar size, each bearing one of the letters on the railcars, but in shuffled order. The cursor is a gloved hand, drawn in Disney cartoon style. As best we can tell, it appears that the object of this children's computer program is to click the mouse on one of the skeleton keys, drag it over to the railcar bearing the same letter, and then click the mouse again as the key reaches its destination. When the correct letter match is made, the door of the railcar opens, revealing an object whose name begins with the same letter.

Kelly, Lucas's mother, stands behind her son. Bouncing his 6-month-old baby sister on her hip, she tries to decipher the object of the game so that she can gently prod Lucas with directions. When the engine pulls across the screen with the letters *A* and *Z*, Kelly says, "Okay. Find a letter, Lucas. Find an *A*." Kelly stays watching him try to maneuver the cursor to one of the keys. Lucas clicks on the one with the *A* and drags it to the matching railcar. It opens, revealing an apple. "What is that?" Kelly asks. "Good! You got it. Now find a *Z*." Lucas clicks on the *Z*. The railcar door opens to reveal a drawing of what we take a few moments to identify as a zipper. From our position, it looks like a drawing of a railroad track. "What is that?" Kelly asks. Lucas's response is more a question than an answer: "A zipper?" he asks. "Right!" exclaims his mother before moving on. Lucas keeps clicking, dragging and matching. "There is an *M* for monkey, a *V* for vegetable, and an *L* for lamb . . . and also for Lucas!" he shouts with glee, turning to his mother to make sure she sees.

Kelly keeps a close eye on Lucas's progress throughout the game, although her direct help is no longer needed. She offers sporadic words of encouragement. "Lucas, you're very good at this." In an aside, she tells us, "I like this kind of game. It's very educational. And then she adds, "He's learning his letters–identifying what they look like and seeing what starts with it. He knows his *A* and *Z* but for a lot of the others he's still guessing. I think he's getting it, though. " She reminds us that he's developing "fine motor coordination" as he moves the mouse without looking at it, and sees the effect this action has on the object on the screen. Her knowledge of Lucas's development might impress even the best reading diagnostician.

By this time, Lucas has been playing on the computer for almost an hour. Patiently his mother has been watching, occupying the baby on her hip for the entire time, while scooting around the library to look for his favorite books. Finally she says, "Lucas, we have to go." He resists: "I'm playing my game!" With negotiation as an everyday part of their interactions, his mother counters: "I'm going to put Ann in her seat. Then we can go home and read *Hi! Pizza Man!*"

It's the promise of the story that entices Lucas to leave the computer.

IN NEIGHBORHOODS OF CONCENTRATED AFFLUENCE, compe-
tition among families is endemic. We see it in the early reading activities,
and now we see it with the computer. The push to learn skills earlier and
better than their peers is evident in every activity. When you watch, it often
seems like the adults intentionally subordinate their own abilities in order
to manipulate greater learning opportunities for their children. We see it in
a grandmother who tells Sophie, age 3, who is playing on the computer,
"I can't do this; can you help me?" Rather than a request, this is really the
grandmother's way of encouraging her granddaughter to take over. As Sophie plays, the grandmother points to pictures on the computer screen, "See,
there's seashells and sand and starfish . . . " using the pictures for an informal
language lesson. Throughout the activity, the grandmother is smiling, sometimes singing along, obviously tremendously proud of Sophie's prowess. Now
independent, Sophie continues with her game, and the grandmother drifts
away to browse among the shelves for books. Along the shelves, she picks
up a brochure entitled "What I Can Do to Help," which offers tips on getting
children to read early, and she reads it intently. Like parent, like grandparent,
the transmission of advantage is evident in her intentionality. When the game
is over, Grandmother immediately routes Sophie to another learning game,
saying, "Do you want shapes or numbers?" "Shapes." "That's a good choice,"
her grandmother says, knowing that either would have suited her goals.

Enacted even in the preschool area, the competition can be fierce for
achievement. Soon Sophie and her grandmother are joined by another
grandmother/granddaughter combination. Casey, age 3, watches Sophie
play, and soon gets restless, saying "I want to play." So the grandmother
turns to Sophie and says "Sophie dear, it is Casey's turn. You get up and
watch her this time. " Casey, too, can maneuver her mouse with facility and
seems very familiar with the games she plays. Sophie watches a few minutes,
then turn to her grandmother and says, "She's slow." Maintaining her cool,
the grandmother says, "Maybe Casey just likes to do it a little more slowly
than you do." (Our research assistant murmurs "ouch" with this one.)

Now the grandmothers get to chatting about their young prodigies' computer skills. "Only three years old and look how well she does on that computer." "I had to teach myself, but I'm learning," says the other grandmother.
"I've been doing the email and I go on websites–you can't get any information anymore unless you go online. But she's so much better than me, and
she's what . . . all of three years old"; and "Just look at how she just sits there
and moves that mouse. I think it's wonderful."

As the interaction continues, the grandparents seem to be competing for the "Best Grandmother of the Year Award" as they assist their grandchildren's learning.

> Grandmother 1: Look, Sophie, that train has the letter T on it. Can you find the letter T?
> Grandmother 2: Look, Casey (as she kneels down and points to the screen). You have to take the train and put it up there. That's it! Good. And the star . . . goes where? Up there? Good job, Casey.

Strikingly, although neither grandmother claims to be computer literate, they seem determined to make sure that their grandchildren are not excluded from any opportunity that might contribute to their advancement. The machine might still be mysterious and formidable, but they are willing to take their chances so that their grandchildren can receive all of its advantages.

THE NUMBERS ARE REVEALING. We return to counting children's activities in the computer areas in each library, the average age of the child, the number of lines of print he or she encounters and whether or not an adult accompanies them in the area. In 2-hour segments at different points in the day, we spend about 40 hours in each library, counting and recording activities.

Here we take out a typical hour in each of the libraries. First, you will note that despite all the bells and whistles in these computer programs, none particularly hold the child's attention very long. In both libraries, children tend to open a program, play a little bit, and move on to another. Second, notice the differences in the lines of print children are likely to read during these play activities. More often, there are no lines of print in the activities for children at Lillian Marrero, while there may be at least one or more in the activities for children at Chestnut Hill. Third, look at whether or not the child is accompanied by an adult, and what that adult might be doing during the play activity. For the children at Chestnut Hill, the adult is likely to be present, assisting, directing, or looking on during the play activities; in contrast, at Lillian Marrero, the child is either likely to be alone, or with an adult who is watching the activities. Finally, note the activity in which the children are engaged; in Chestnut Hill, activities center around numbers and letters; in Lillian Marrero, they center around games.

These patterns become even more revealing in Table 4.3, a summary of all of our hours of observation. Starting early, children are using the computers for learning activities in Chestnut Hill at a much younger age than those at Lillian Marrero. Here we can see stark differences in the average age of the child playing with these applications; at Lillian Marrero the average age is

Table 4.1. An Example of Preschool Computer Activity: Chestnut Hill

Gender/ Age	Computer Activity	Time	Lines of Print	Companion/ Relationship	Companion Activity	Time
F/6	Millie's Math House (numbers)	3:25–3:37	1	with C/m/6 (brother)	assisting	3:25–3:37
M/5	Millie's Math House (numbers)	3:37–3:40	1	alone		
		3:40–3:50	1	with AA/m/5	assisting	3:40–3:50
	Millie's Math House (shapes)	3:50–3:58	0	with AA/m/5	assisting	3:50–3:58
F/3	Reader Rabbit Toddler (letters)	4:40–4:42	1	alone		
F/3	Reader Rabbit Toddler (letters)	4:42–4:44	1	Caregiver	assisting	4:42–4:44
		4:44–4:50	1	alone		
M/2	RR Toddler (letters)	4:55–5:15	1	Cauc/f/30 (mother)	demonstrating	4:55– 5:10
				AA/m/2 (peer)	watching	5:05–5:10
				AA/f/35 Other adult	assisting	5:05–5:10
F/3	RR Toddler (letters)	5:18–5:22	1	Cauc/f/30	assisting	5:18–5:22

Table 4.2. An Example of Preschool Computer Activity: Lillian Marrero

Gender/ Age	Computer Activity	Time	Lines of Print	Companion/ Relationship	Companion Activity	Time
F/8	Reader Rabbit (coloring)	2:45–3:00	0	alone		
	Reader Rabbit (coloring)	3:00–3:06	0	AA/m/8 (peer)	distracting	3:00–3:06
M/8	Reader Rabbit (coloring)	2:55–2:58	0	alone		
	Reader Rabbit (coloring)	2:58–3:10	0	AA/m/8 (peer)	distracting	2:58–3:10
F/6	Reader Rabbit (numbers)	3:09–3:15	1	alone		
	Reader Rabbit (coloring)	3:15–3:32	0	AA/m/8	watching	3:15–3:32
	Kidspiration (coloring)	3:32–3:36	0			
	Reader Rabbit (numbers)	3:36–3:41	1	alone		
	Reader Rabbit (coloring)	3:41–3:55	0			
	Green Eggs & Ham (game)	3:55–4:00	0			
	Reader Rabbit Toddler (game)	4:00–4:01	0			
	Timon & Pumba (game)	4:01–4:02	0			
M/6	Millie's Math House	4:10–4:30	1	alone		
	Millies' Math House (numbers)	4:30–4:35	1	alone		
		4:35–4:40	0	alone		
M/8	Curious George (game)	4:40–5:00	0	AA/m/9 (peer)	watching	4:40–5:00
		5:00–5:10		alone		
		5:10–5:20		AA/m/10 (peer)	watching	5:10–5:20
F/12	Curious George (game)	5:15–5:20	0	alone		

Table 4.3. A Summary Table of Preschool Computer Activity at Libraries

	Lillian Marrero	**Chestnut Hill**
Average age	7.2 years	3.1 years
Average time with adult/caregiver (Assisting, directing, watching)	.23 minutes	3.9 minutes
Average time spent with material containing print	5.6 minutes	10.1 minutes

7; in Chestnut Hill, 3. Parental attention is also dramatically different across the two settings, with the Chestnut Hill child likely to receive about 17 times more attention than the Lillian Marrero child. Finally, even with the modest amount of print in many of these applications, Chestnut Hill children are likely to spend about twice the amount of time with material containing print than their counterparts at Lillian Marrero.

RETURNING TO OUR THEORY OF ACTION, what might these patterns reveal about the promise of technology for leveling the playing field? If we look at previous technology innovations, the patterns are troubling. Take, for example, the 1969 debut of *Sesame Street,* a show that was specifically designed to narrow readiness disparities as part of President Johnson's War on Poverty. Through the brilliance of Joan Ganz Cooney and her colleagues, *Sesame Street* concocted a formula that figured out how children at an early age could become familiar with letters and sounds as they delighted in the foibles of Bert and Ernie. You might recall the wonderful double entendres, the catchy lyrics, and the big-name stars who would suddenly pop up on your screen spouting the ABCs, enthralling young children as well as their parents. Apparently, though, the show attracted some parents more than others. A series of studies (Ball & Bogatz, 1970; Bogatz & Ball, 1971) revealed that middle-class parents used the program to engage their little ones in learning activities of letters and numbers, while lower-income parents allowed their children to watch on their own. Subsequent evaluations of the program (Cook et al., 1975), in fact, showed evidence of actually increasing differences in achievement, helping those children who were already somewhat prepared for formal reading instruction far more than the less-ready children, who benefited little from the show. As a result of the program, studies (Goldsen, 1977) found larger gaps in skills by kindergarten for middle- and low-income neighborhood children than ever before.

Television, however, is a relatively passive medium. Although children can actively watch, the medium can't adjust or modify its content to meet their individual needs. Now take a technology that is truly interactive, such as computer software, and look at its potential for early reading skills. Early reading skills, particularly the first part of the reading equation–phonological awareness (rhyming, alliteration, segmenting, and blending) and letter name knowledge–are especially well-suited to the mastery learning capabilities of the computer. With adult supervision, computer programs, specially orchestrated to drill and practice these skills, can make the work like play, in a manner that builds both speed and fluency. Consequently, what would ordinarily be a centerpiece in kindergarten is now in the hands of a miraculous machine and an authoritative parent who is guiding his or her child at age 3.

When you take out the drudgery part of the reading process–learning the basic decoding skills–and make them automatic, you provide working memory capacity to do other things, such as thinking about what you read in the text. This is the fun part of the reading process because it allows you to learn and develop knowledge that will be critical for the second part of the reading equation–comprehension. In some respect, then, the sooner a child can learn about the nuts and bolts of reading, the sooner he or she can begin to build a knowledge base and become an independent learner–and the sooner, too, that the child can build the conceptual base that will be critical for the development of information capital.

Before this time of independence, however, children will need adult assistance in learning about reading and learning to read. In this environment in which the playing field was somewhat level, our observations made plain

Children at Computer Playing

the centrality of adult scaffolding–even with these so-called self-teaching programs. There was a power dynamic that differed across settings. In one setting, the power seemed to be held by the parent, who manipulated the tools to their children's learning advantage. In the other setting, the power balance seemed to favor the tool, with the parent deferring to its will, and allowing the child to take ownership. This relationship seemed to hold true regardless of whether the tool was a book or a computer.

In fact, there were striking similarities in the patterns of parental behaviors across book reading and computer activities. For parents in Chestnut Hill, computers seem to represent a new competitive tool to drive their young child toward greater competence and achievement. In our observations, it was virtually the norm, not the exception, for parents to use the programs to drill (through computer play) children in letters, sounds, and numbers. For parents in the Badlands, computer use was at the whim of the child and his or her interests. Most often, this would mean either rather frenetic play, with multiple applications attempted then dropped, or advancing toward the end of the program to reach the games that were designed to serve as rewards for learning. In either case, computers were used as play without their concomitant learning advantages.

Throughout our observations, therefore, we see pernicious signs that the very tool designed to level the playing field, is in fact, un-leveling it. With parents in an affluent community like Chestnut Hill relentlessly pursuing every advantage for their children, computers provide yet another tool toward advancement, a little prep school in a machine to enable their young ones to get ahead. Living in this highly charged competitive environment, children will come to school already knowing the key components of early reading. With parents in a community like the Badlands, struggling with poverty and its effects, computers provide a diversion from other activities, perhaps a respite from the limited options available in their community. Consequently, these children will need more of the traditional fare that kindergarten provides, much-needed practice on the fundamentals of decoding. And while these children are working toward becoming fluent in the first part of the reading equation–learning to read–their affluent peers will be on the second part of the reading equation–reading to learn. In short, the not-so-small disparities in skills for children of affluence and children of poverty are about to get ever larger. Rather than contain the Matthew Effect, the digital technology might just be accelerating it.

CHAPTER 5

The More, the More
(The Less, the Less)

As the most sophisticated and powerful tool devised by humans, the greatest potential of computers is to liberate brainpower. Computers have the capacity to speed up automatic processes to allow people to tackle problems hitherto considered impossible. One computer can make more calculations in an hour than a Yankee Stadium full of scientists can make in a person's lifetime. A small laptop can multiply 500,000 ten-digit numbers in a single second. Mental operations that could once overwhelm working memory can be efficiently stored, giving us freedom to engage in abstract reasoning, problem-solving, and the capacity to acquire new knowledge. Their potential for expanding the horizons of young students and for offering new tools for learning is truly extraordinary.

Nevertheless, historically, each new medium of mass communication within a few years of its introduction has met with increasing skepticism, condemned as a threat to the young people who use it the most (DeFleur & Ball-Rokeach, 1989). In the past, it might have been comics, radio, movies, or the telephone. Today, critics blame cell phones, digital toys, and computer-based games for capturing excessive time and interest of youth. Perhaps the most popular thesis is that it displaces or takes time away from such intellectually demanding activities such as reading or homework. Naysayers assume the dreaded medium has a homogenous effect on all who use it, captivating students with a level of engagement that is close to addiction. This happens, according to the thesis, because the new media are simply more attractive to students, presumably more so than other activities. Not only might it displace concurrent activities and learning opportunities, but extensive experience might lead to enduring habits of use that are intellectually passive.

It is this premise—and the computer's capacity to potentially support or derail reading—that led us to examine the next step in our theory of action. Because once students have developed basic decoding skills, they will need to practice and to read voluminously. Simply reading anything will not suffice, however. Rather, they will need to tackle challenging texts to rapidly build up their word and world knowledge. Computers and their capabilities can potentially stimulate this process, exposing students to multiple texts and many different genres. Alternatively, they can distract from reading by providing other, more rewarding, options. The questions we raised in this chapter, therefore, were: Do computers help or hinder the amount and quality of reading activity? Might they motivate students to read more, particularly for those students who have not had the benefits of adult mentoring in the early years? Do they displace or transform reading activity?

Similar to our previous chapter, we once again look back before we look forward. First, we examine reading trends for students in these critical middle years, before technology has been integrated in these libraries. Our rationale is to try to avoid the techno-centric argument: namely, the view that students would read if only technology wasn't so distracting. We then fast-forward to examine reading activity right after technology is in place, and then once again, when the novelty has worn off. We look at the continuities and discontinuities in reading through different media. Next, we examine current uses of books and computers for these tweens in the libraries, comparing and contrasting across our two neighborhoods, and how these activities might interact with students' approaches to homework, presumably tied to skill development. Finally, we describe patterns and media habits that appear to forecast the further development of information capital for students as they use these increasingly sophisticated tools for learning.

WHEN PEOPLE THINK ABOUT children's development, they typically consider the first 5 years of life. Although these early years are marked by striking changes, the developmental and social changes that occur from ages 10 through 13 are dramatic as well. During these years, children make strides toward adulthood by becoming competent, independent, and involved in worlds beyond their families and immediate neighbors. In these middle childhood years, children will develop an expectation of whether they will succeed or fail at different tasks, an orientation toward achievement that will color their response to learning.

Especially in the earliest phases of middle childhood, children will work toward developing the second part of the reading equation in the "simple view"–language comprehension. Although it might appear that reading development should just be a matter of decoding letter strings fluently into words, reading achievement is about making meaning. The relationship of skills is multiplicative $(R = D \times C)$: you can't have one without the other. Even if a child has perfect ability in one area, like decoding (a score of 1), but completely fails in the other area, comprehension (a score of 0), the child will not be able to read well.

Studies (e.g, Chall, Jacobs, & Baldwin, 1990) tend to confirm that age 8 is a pivotal year for these skills to come together. This is when young students typically transition from learning to read to reading to learn. Children will increasingly read difficult texts independently and will have to rely on self-teaching strategies to comprehend the text. Reading new words in texts, students gain some rudimentary ideas about the word's meaning through the context of what they are reading. Over time and with multiple encounters, they will gradually learn the word's denotations and connotations and its modes of use. By the time they reach 12th grade, high-performing students will have learned about 60,000 to 80,000 words, not by direct instruction in school but by accruing bits of word knowledge for each of the thousands they read each day.

Given the staggering number of new words that students will need to add to their vocabularies each year, school time alone can't possibly provide the time students will need to become proficient readers. Rather, they will need to read voraciously, outside of school. The process of reading to learn depends on students having extended periods of time immersed in highly challenging but achievable reading experiences. Consequently, the potential displacement of book reading could have serious implications not only for the future of print as a medium for enjoyment and learning, but for developing the second phase of reading acquisition. That is, of course, unless students are using computers to accumulate or potentially even accelerate their understandings of words, concepts, and information.

WE BEGAN OUR ANALYSIS of tween reading right after the computers came to the libraries in the late 1990s. Recognizing that these young students often engage in many different activities in relatively short periods of time, we decided to change our time sampling methodology to take quick written "snapshots" of reading behavior in student areas of each library using a momentary time-sampling strategy. Working together as a team, two research assistants would observe a student for 30 seconds, report on a behavior, whether it was reading in a book or on a computer, rest for 10 seconds, and then observe the next child for 30 seconds. From this initial analysis, we sorted their various activities into three generic behaviors: reading (listening to text being read, including by the computer; reading by self; reading to another person); literacy-related activity (writing, typing, skimming over text, talking about text, browsing, looking at pictures in books or on computers); and other (wandering around, waiting, staring into space). We conducted five sets of observations, each 2 hours in length. These data were then translated into percentages of time spent on behaviors in each area in the library.

Several years later in 2002, once the novelty of the technology wore off, we conducted the study again using the same observational methods. Once we gathered all the data, we created a summary chart of reading activity to examine the potential displacement of reading.

Figure 5.1 on the next page shows that reading activity was relatively similar in both libraries right after technology was introduced. Tweens in Chestnut Hill spent about 15% of their time reading compared to tweens in Lillian Marrero, who spent 14% of the time reading. There was, however, a fair amount of time in both libraries devoted to literacy-related activities. This might involve talking about books, writing, browsing, or looking at pictures in a book. In both libraries, there was also a fair amount of time devoted to hanging around—meeting friends, talking, and engaging in general social activities.

Now take a look at Figure 5.2, which shows what happens several years later. For young students in Chestnut Hill, technology did not replace reading; in fact, the amount of time spent on the computer reading increased significantly, almost doubling what it was before. However, you could also argue that technology did not replace reading for young students in Lillian Marrero. There was not much time spent reading initially with the introduction of technology, and not much time devoted to reading activity later on. In other words, the technology, with its motivational capabilities and flexibility of use, did not seem to support greater attention to reading print. Neither did it draw them away, however, from something they had done before.

What we did find, more often in Lillian Marrero than in Chestnut Hill, is a greater amount of time spent hanging around. As one librarian found, "Books are something you look at while you wait for a computer." Almost like an arcade, groups of students tend to gather around the person on the computer, who is typically playing games of all varieties. Sometimes the crowds could be so unwieldy as to drive adults and other seniors to leave the library.

In these two graphs, however, you will notice another phenomenon: The gap in the amount of time spent reading between young students in these communities has increased substantially. Aligned with what we saw more broadly in Chapter 3, regardless of technology (printed text in books or computers), reading tends to predominate in Chestnut Hill where it does not in Lillian Marrero. Consequently, after years of technology improvements, there is now a larger gap in the amount of time spent on the activity between these two communities than before. In fact, based on our rough estimates of the number of words read over the course of these observations, we calculated 35,815 words at Chestnut Hill compared to 16,396 words at Lillian Marrero, almost a 2:1 ratio.

GIVEN THE INTEGRATION OF MEDIA, displacement may take subtler forms today than one medium merely replacing another. As we have already seen, one can read effectively on computers or in e-books instead of traditional printed texts. In other words, new media can transform a particular

Figure 5.1. Percentage of Time Spent on Activities: Right After Technology (1998)

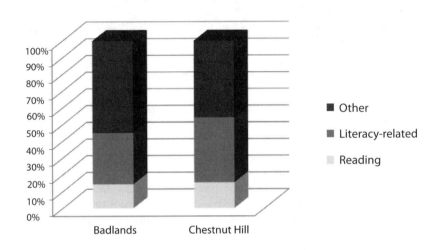

Figure 5.2. Percentage of Time Spent on Activities: Several Years Later (2002)

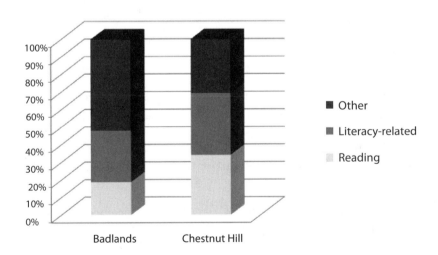

activity rather than displace it. Therefore, an important key to understanding how technology may transform reading and the development of information capital is to understand how a medium is used—its purposes and functions.

Exploring this area, we find factors that may influence learners' preconceptions about the medium and the mental effort they engage in when processing the medium. It has been proposed that learners' preconceptions of the amount of mental effort invested in an activity influences the quantity and quality of information gained. In a series of groundbreaking studies, for example, Gabriel Salomon (1984) found that the experience of watching television seemed to engender the general impression of something that is easy to assimilate. In turn, the impression caused a decrease in the amount of mental effort, the number of nonautomatic elaborations applied to a unit of material. Researchers (Beentjes, 1989) explain the empirical finding by arguing that the comprehension of television "texts" tends to be significantly lower than the comprehension of written texts. From this view, reading books is a superior medium since it requires greater mental effort and results in greater learning.

This theory of displacement (Neuman, 1995) led us to investigate how tweens in our two libraries used each medium, 5 years after our first study of displacement. Here we take a look specifically at each medium separately and the type of materials that are used; for example, whether or not students look at entertaining materials on computers, such as games, movies, or information sources, and similar categories for materials in print. In Table 5.1 you will see an example of how we examined and coded these activities, focusing on the reading area and the computer area in each library.

Summaries of these activities are described in Tables 5.2 and 5.3. In contrast to Salomon's thesis, we find a very different pattern of media use. Students' media patterns tend to reflect more similarities than differences. For example, students at Lillian Marrero tend to read print materials that are entertaining and easy; we find a pattern of reading/browsing puzzle books and books on entertainment figures and games. Similarly, when they are on the computers, they are likely to spend time on entertaining websites, watching movies or game-like shows. In contrast, Chestnut Hill students spend 12 times the amount of time on informational reading materials in print; similarly, they spend about 5 times as much time on informational texts on computers. Our very rough calculation suggests that about 39% of these informational activities relate to homework for students in Chestnut Hill, versus about 9% in Lillian Marrero.

What we see, then, are habits of use that tend to be more intellectually active or relatively passive. Studies of other media, such as television viewing, have proposed that heavy doses of "entertaining" experiences lead to mental laziness, an unwillingness to invest the mental effort required to

Table 5.1. Examples of Momentary Time Sampling in the Library

Child	1	2	3	4	5	6	7	8	9	10
Activity setting: Children's tables										
Female 1	1	1	1	1	1					
Male 1	2	2–3	2	2–3	2					

Brief description of activity: Female 1 reads an adult-sized storybook. Male 1 appears to be with tutor. Female 2 fills out her reading sheet, then leaves for computer section.

Activity setting: Computers										
Female 2	2–3	2–3	2	2	2					
Child	1	2	3	4	5	6	7	8	9	10
Male 1	3	3	3	3	2					
Male 2	2	2–3	3	2–3–2	2					

Brief description of activity: Male 1 and Male 2 playing game together

Legend:
1: Reading (read to self, listen to text read, read to other person)
2: Literacy related (write/type, scroll, flip, surf, look at pictures)
3: Other (space out, wander, wait)

Table 5.2. Time Spent Reading Texts in Libraries for Tweens (10–12 years old)

Students	Badlands	Chestnut Hill
Average number of minutes reading per student	14.8	33.6
Average number of minutes with entertainment reading materials per student	21.5	13.3
Average number of minutes with informational reading materials per student	1.25	12.0
Average number of items read per student	1.06	1.57
Average number of minutes reading observed per hour in library	14.8	26.6
Total hours of observation	24	24

Table 5.3. Time Spent Reading on Computers in Libraries for Tweens (10–12 years old)

Students	Badlands	Chestnut Hill
Average number of minutes reading per student	18 minutes	28 minutes
Average number of minutes with entertainment reading materials per child	14.2 minutes	4.3 minutes
Average number of minutes with informational reading materials per child	4.6 minutes	23.7 minutes
Total hours of observation	24	24

master reading and informational text. Contrary to this view, however, our findings seem to suggest that it is the individual—not the medium—that drives the action. In Chestnut Hill, students use media more for information purposes than for entertainment; in the Badlands, it is the other way around. Strikingly, these patterns seem to mirror the parental patterns with media and the ways in which they interacted with their young children, as shown in previous chapters.

In summary, we do not find a typical pattern of displacement—that computers take away the time that would normally be spent reading. This assumes that the medium is in charge. Rather, we find that it is the individual who takes advantage of the medium. In Chestnut Hill, this translates into more reading and more attention to informational text in books and computer activity. In the Badlands, we find little change in the amount of time spent reading. Computers do not displace reading. More likely they take time away from literacy-related conversations by engaging larger numbers of people in game-like activities. Time spent with both media for students in the Badlands community is focused more on entertainment than information, suggesting that habits of use may cut across different media. Finally, it is clear that new media do not have a homogeneous use and effect among our younger generation, and that the sometimes draconian prediction of technology taking over the lives of our children has been overly dramatized. Clearly the students are in charge and not the medium.

HOMEWORK MAY NOT BE ON THE TOP OF THE LIST for young tweens as a preferable after-school activity. Still, we know that by completing homework and turning it in on time, students can learn important lessons about discipline, responsibility, and communication. They can also practice and review important skills that they have learned in school and improve their reading time practice and academic achievement.

Therefore, we turned our attention to homework, an activity that drives many students into the library in the afternoon, to examine how the technology might influence homework activities. Conceivably, it might turn a somewhat unattractive activity into a more interesting and constructive event. However, the compelling nature of the computer might draw students farther away from the worksheets, drills, and computations that often seem de rigueur in these middle childhood years.

Lessons from previous innovations in technology here are instructive. Previous research had once presumed that television displaced homework activities. As the assumption went, television, the more attractive medium, might replace the rather dull and repetitive task of completing homework. However, psychologist Dan Anderson and his colleagues (Anderson & Collins, 1988) found this not to be the case. Their studies indicated that students were not spending much time on homework before television was ubiquitous in American homes, and they are still not spending time on it today. At the same time, they noted the beginnings of a trend that has since become a common phenomenon: multitasking. Students completed their limited homework activities while watching television. In fact, survey data (Arafeh, Levin, Rainie, & Lenhart, 2010) indicate that tweens reportedly multitask "most of the time," and about 25% report watching television or talking with friends while they do their homework.

As the newer media come to occupy students' attention, some speculate that multitasking will increase, leading students to engage in using multiple media simultaneously. Concerns about the media's effects on students' cognition, particularly their attention skills and attentional styles, have been the subject of considerable debate. As a result, we decided to examine how homework might be influenced by these changes in technology. Since each of our libraries sponsored LEAP, an after-school program that provides homework assistance, computer literacy, and multicultural enrichment activities to students daily, 4:00 p.m. and beyond is a busy time in both libraries. We decided to spend 5 consecutive days in each library, watching how homework is enacted, getting a sense of the rhythm and activities that engage students during these afternoon hours, and whether or not computers are displacing homework or creating an even greater cacophony of multitasking activities.

In relation to homework activities, the library often acts like a strict parent. "Homework must come first," according to the afternoon policies in each library. LEAP leaders and their assistants are highly visible to ensure that this is the case. In this respect, our setting for examining homework is far more constrained than what might normally occur in the home without direct supervision. Nevertheless, the co-occurrence of having an afternoon program targeted to homework help in each library allowed us to compare

Socializing at the Library

and contrast homework enactment in each community, and potentially determine whether there are commonalities or differences in displacement.

Unlike our previous analyses, however, homework time defies easy counts and frequencies. Rather, you need to observe how homework is enacted among tweens. Although we might hope that students are consciously spending hours after school working on homework, the actual practice is far different. This is what it looks like.

At 4:00 p.m. at Lillian Marrero library, the gentle hum of the few people speaking in quiet tones turns into a wild orchestration of voices as 50 tweens enter the library all at once. Suddenly, every computer station is occupied, with the remaining 40 seats taken at each of the nine reading tables. Snacks come out; worksheets appear, cell phones are briefly examined to be returned to their backpack before any librarians take notice. Elaine Kumpf, who oversees the LEAP program here, stops to greet each student and to ask if they need any help. Most of the students are chatting with friends, some doing worksheets together while a few are working alone. Occasionally, a student might run up to Kumpf with a question but most work independently.

The setting looks like a social network; students circulate among other tables, share the latest gossip with one another, and give old friends special hugs. Clusters of teens hang around, often waiting to get on the computer. Despite the policy and despite the enforcement, after about five minutes nary a homework assignment appears in view.

The noise is a bit deafening, and one girl who is trying to complete an assignment asks Kumpf if she can use some headphones. Although it's against library policy, Kumpf tries to accommodate her and retrieves some from the office. The girl adjusts the headphones for comfort and then returns to work. Even from where we sit, about 6 feet away, we can hear the music blasting from the headphones. Every few minutes the music ends, then she clicks on the music website, searches for a new song, clicks back to the window for her homework assignment and resumes taking notes. She does this at least four times. Back and forth, she effortlessly moves from one site to another.

It is close to 4:45 p.m., and an assistant glances over at the girl. For the first time, she notices the headphones and music. Bounding up from her chair, she stands directly behind the girl to take a closer look. "Are you doing your homework?" she asks in an accusatory tone. Pausing slowly, Sara lifts the headphone from just one ear, turns her head, and leans over her right shoulder to looks squarely at the aide. "Sure," and resumes her soft singing and copying.

The scene isn't all that different at the Chestnut Hill library. At 2:45 p.m., the library is virtually empty; by 4:00 p.m., you cannot find a seat in the library. What starts as a trickle of students coming in by twos and threes turns into a rush, with groups of students eventually taking over every seat at the tables and computers, as well as overwhelming the stacks. Presumably here for "homework help," students of all ages and races cluster around tables, all talking at once, save for one or two students who are reading.

Here, the sacred hour of "homework comes first" is held with lesser force by Dunia Kravchak, the LEAP coordinator, an exotically striking woman in her 20s. Games of chess, checkers, and monopoly await the students after finishing their homework, although this is hardly the rule. Jalen, a 2nd grader, immediately walks in and sits down at the chess board without opening his homework. His buddy, 12-year-old Joshua, walks by to see what his friend is up to. Jalen asks him to play a game. "Can't–I've got to do my homework," Joshua tells him. He returns to the computer station. In literally seconds, he reconsiders his options, picks up his open textbook, and carries it back to the chess game. He sets the open textbook next to the board, and ponders his move in the game. Kravchak spots Joshua's open textbook. "You have homework?" He nods sheepishly. "Go do your homework and I'll take your place," suggests Kravchak. Joshua grabs his textbook, goes back to his place, while she slides into the vacant seat temporarily. He returns to the game in less than 10 minutes.

These scenes, and indeed they are scenes, are what you're likely to see consistently on an average day in both libraries. It is multitasking–not with one medium, but with many different activities that all appear to engage these tweens simultaneously. Whether it is social activities, music, games, or competing websites, it seems to have the same effect: Tweens rarely seem to concentrate on one activity at a time, despite the most rigid of rules in the library.

Although studies suggest that multitasking is not a particularly effective strategy (Willingham, 2010), this message doesn't seem to concern these students. In fact, we see two forms of multitasking: One is synchronous; the other, asynchronous. We see many of the students listening to music while they are presumably hard at work on their homework. While the research literature is not definitive on whether this may help or hinder performance, the blaring sounds from iPods suggest that it might be better attuned to patterned routines than creative endeavors. We also see asynchronous multitasking, or switching between two tasks. Switching involves short bursts of involvement between two tasks. According to cognitive psychologist Daniel Willingham (2010), it turns out that switching is even more difficult than synchronous multitasking since it requires students to take on different rules and different types of responses. Going from a website on Benjamin Hooks to a search strategy for a music video calls for a student to mentally calibrate to these different circumstances. Neither approach to multitasking is optimal for learning.

In short, our observations seem to highlight more commonalities than differences among students from our two communities when it comes to

Tweens at the Computer

homework. Although Chestnut Hill students spend more time with information text that might be related to schoolwork than those in the Badlands, neither group of students seems to take homework assignments particularly seriously. It is a task to complete, not necessarily a task to learn from.

Typically, research in technologies and new media assume that increases in time for one medium (such as computers and the Internet) will logically mean decreases in the time given to other activities (Beentjes & Van der Voort, 1988). The concern, of course, is that activities like homework, which are essential to learning, will be sacrificed in favor of other more pleasurable activities. But this is not the case with homework. Students, with guidance, support, and regulation from LEAP leaders, do complete their assignments. They just engage in other, more immediate pleasurable activities simultaneously. Rather than displace homework, these other activities actively interfere with the mental effort that might otherwise go into a more thoughtful and more challenging activity. Whether it is the assignment given or how the assignment is enacted, not much learning appears to accrue from these activities.

In essence, the patterns that we recorded throughout the years, right after technology entered the less novel phase of its existence to the present time, seem to suggest that media are put to an individual's use rather than the other way around. Students' uses of the computer in Chestnut Hill hold striking resemblance to their uses of printed text. Similarly, we find no major shifts in students' uses of media for those who live in the Badlands. Rather than displace other more constructive activities, media habits seem to complement one another. Those seeking information are likely to do so in print and computers; others, seeking entertainment, are likely to use media to serve these needs as well. Therefore, neither the pessimistic projections of computers taking over more worthwhile activities, nor the optimistic forecasters who predict that this technology might break down the barriers of missed opportunities and limited resources, appear to accurately characterize their uses for students in these neighborhoods.

Given the variations across communities in media patterns, it is clear that the prognosticators who hold technology responsible for captivating the tween generation with a level of passive engagement leading to mental laziness and for generating indiscriminate fascination with all its messages have assumed that media have a homogenous use and effect. This is not the case. Technology's influence is in the hand of the user. And for students who have been carefully tutored early in life on its uses, technology may serve as a tool for learning; for others, unfortunately, it may only be a respite from it.

Despite the context of being in the library, neither group spent much time on independent reading. Students might place a book a two before themselves, but the social activity seemed to be more of the driving force than the reading activity. Although the opportunities to read challenging and diverse materials were clearly available, tweens appeared to be interested in other things. It provides a striking reminder that while the environment may play a vital role in development and encourage certain behavior, it cannot determine behavior.

Therefore, in contrast to the view that computers might be able to pick up the slack for those who might not want to engage in reading practice, our findings are discouraging. For it appears that students who are inclined to read for information, challenging themselves with more difficult texts, are likely to do so in either medium; similarly, those who wish to avoid such experiences follow their muse regardless of the medium, playing out the final chords of the Matthew Effect, or what we call "the more, the more (the less, the less)." Despite its enormous capabilities, the digital revolution cannot seem to overcome the differences and reciprocal influences of early experiences with print for children and families in these communities.

This disparity in the amount of reading has many other consequences for students besides their future reading comprehension and performance. Reading a lot serves to develop knowledge bases, the first mode of reasoning associated with information capital. Students are likely to come in contact with the vocabulary, text structures, and complex sentence patterns that are characteristic of academic texts, and the language of school and higher education. Unlike conversational vocabulary, which is often limited and re-petitive, written vocabulary includes a larger corpus of words, many of which occur infrequently, which may be learned in context. Words in these con-texts play a particularly critical role in communicating ideas more precisely.

The subsequent exercise of the reading habit leads to more rapid, ex-tensive, and automatic processing, increasing the amount of reading and the knowledge you are likely to acquire. Upper elementary and middle school texts, for example, are often jam-packed with content-specific vocabulary, concepts, and information. Therefore, the number of words, and precise new meanings of these words in multiple and different contexts, are likely to build increasingly complex knowledge networks. Having some knowledge predicts more knowledge. For example, Donna Recht and Lauren Leslie (1988) con-ducted an experiment to examine the effects of prior knowledge and native ability. These researchers worked with high- and low-knowledge 7th graders. Students were given a baseball text passage and asked to reenact the action described in the story, summarize the text, and sort sentences from the pas-sage in terms of their importance. On each and every measure students with greater knowledge of baseball recalled more than those with less knowledge. General ability did not lead to capability in any of these tasks; rather, it was prior knowledge that was the crucial factor in determining performance.

The development of information capital, therefore, goes beyond the Matthew Effect to describe how reading relates to real-life issues, affecting day-to-day decision making. This has led us to posit the knowledge gap hy-pothesis (Neuman & Celano, 2006). Reading a lot helps to develop knowl-edge networks, or schemas that act like what Donald Rumelhart (1980) describes as the "building blocks of cognition." Schemas provide students with the conceptual apparatus for making sense of the world around them by classifying these incoming bits of information into similar groups, and ever-enlarging knowledge networks. Nancy Stein and Christine Glenn (1979), for example, provided a compelling case for schemas and their usefulness for recalling information from stories. They found that students who read many narratives seemed to internalize a form of story grammar which aided in their understanding and retelling stories. If you are a fan of *Law and Order* like one of us, you'll know exactly how it works. In the first few minutes, the problem is introduced; soon the sage-like police officers are fingering a po-tential suspect who is soon to be revealed not to have committed the crime; lawyers get involved around 20 minutes into the program, and together they discover that the real criminal is some rich, powerful person. The introduc-tion, plot, series of events, and resolution might vary but the structure is the same. Similarly, schemas have been shown to aid in remembering, recalling, and classifying particular entities into similar groups, building through ana-logical reasoning a greater repertoire of knowledge.

But what is particularly important in the process of knowledge acquisition is that schemas provide a kind of organizational prosthetic that serves to diminish the information-processing load. Consider, for example, going to a football game for the first time. It is probably a complex and confusing new world. Not only are there complex rules to consider, but the subtleties of the game strategy, different positions for various players, and roles and routines of the coaches and the crowd, may look like a free-for-all to the uninitiated. As the novice comes to know more about the game, and the schemas of how it works, she begins to form a mental representation of certain activities, devoting less mental energy to the structure of the activity than to the content itself. Certain activities that were originally confusing then become understandable, familiar, and easier to access.

By diminishing the information-processing load, individuals are able to acquire new information more rapidly. Understanding the basic concept of a football game, for example, enables a person to quickly make new associations, creating additional schemas that become increasingly differentiated with more knowledge. Soon she may begin to recognize the subtleties in offensive and defensive strategies, the reasons for one player replacing another, and the nuances of various plays, resulting in greater speed for gathering and remembering information. Knowledge becomes easier to access, producing more knowledge networks.

Conversely, it becomes more difficult to acquire new knowledge when you have little of it. A vicious cycle occurs. Knowledge disparities grow as a result of these differences in the amount, rate, and speed of gathering information from multiple media and resources. The information "haves" are likely to read more and engage with others in more higher-level conversations, creating greater existing pools of knowledge. Greater use of information, in turn, enhances the speed of information acquisition and developing schemas, which over time is likely to accelerate a knowledge gap with "haves" having a lot of knowledge, and "have-nots" much less so. In this case, the have-nots certainly gain knowledge; it is just that the haves gain it all that much faster. And by gaining it faster, they are able to widely outstrip their competition, who may be seeking limited resources or more specialized opportunities.

From this standpoint, media habits established in these formative years resulting in differential practice with reading create differences in the speed of information gathering and knowledge acquisition. As the information flow increases, it will be harder and harder for those who lack reading fluency to keep up. Consequently, the patterns that we see emerging in these two neighborhoods of Chestnut Hill and the Philadelphia Badlands appear to act like an invisible wall, keeping each group insulated from one another, slowly creating a divide that will be difficult to cross over.

CHAPTER 6

The New Literacies

Into the equation enters the Internet, the ultimate platform for accelerating the flow of information. As the fastest-growing form of media, the Internet has no competitor, pushing many other forms of media into obsolescence. Today, the sheer quantity of mediated information that comes across the web has increased by an order of magnitude from about 100 mediated words per minute in 1960 to about 1,000 words per minute in 2007 (Neuman, 2010) available at any time in any place. Information is there for the taking; the question is, however, for whom.

Although the prospect of having facts available at your fingertips may appear to be an astonishing advance for solving the knowledge gap, there are some complications in the process. First, there are some technical aspects of the Internet you need to learn. Reading on the Internet represents the confluence of language and technology—or new literacies—and requires specialized skills for accessing, producing, and making rapid-fire responses (Leu, Kinzer, Coiro, & Cammack, 2000). Using a complex intertwined set of symbols, icons, audio, and virtual reality environments, this style of reading tends to put efficiency and immediacy above all else. Second, the sheer breadth of information flow from any Internet search requires students to develop a discerning eye. In other words, you have to be your own personal reference librarian to filter the reliable information from digital flotsam. Students, therefore, are likely to be challenged by this virtual fire hose of online content, and will need to develop critical reading skills. They will have to learn when to stop clicking and when to start thinking.

The Internet becoming ubiquitous in the libraries raised important implications for our theory of action. On the positive side, the Internet clearly provides tremendous opportunities for learning. Two key theories support this potential. One is that multiple media (e.g., video and print) can enhance word learning and concept development through a synergistic relationship (Neuman, 2009). Combining verbal and visual content (words and pictures) gives learners multiple pathways to retention and comprehension. For example, Richard Mayer and his colleagues (2001) have demonstrated in a series of studies that the addition of moving images, diagrams, and pictures allow for better retention than information held in only one memory system. The

**The New
Literacies**

second is Allan Paivio's dual coding theory (2008), which posits that visual and verbal information are processed differently, creating separate representations for information processed in each channel. In this respect, two channels of information are better than one.

On the negative side, the reading demands of these new literacies and the speed of information coming at you may be overwhelming to the less-practiced reader. Facile use of the Internet involves a complicated set of requirements in addition to the cognitive demands of reading (Coiro & Dobler, 2007). For example, you need to get around the keyboard quickly, and have relatively good spelling and typing skills. You need to juggle multiple texts and different windows. You must carefully define your search terms to avoid being literally overwhelmed with options.

At the same time, no one can doubt the motivational aspects of the Internet and participatory culture it promotes for traditional and nontraditional students alike. Therefore, although the Internet may be redefining everyday discourse with its online world of Twitter and text messaging where acronyms, assorted shortcuts, and creative punctuation have become the norm, one could conceivably argue that its multiple formats might be more amenable to our multitasking students and young adults, and therefore promote knowledge and information capital.

Yet you will see in this chapter that our analysis of the Internet's potential is thwarted by an unexpected factor that impacts students' travels along the so-called information highway. For to become proficient in any skill, including using the Internet, you need not only access to computers but time—time to navigate the medium and to exploit its resources in ways that take full advantage of its options. In our analysis, we will show you how time has become a critical factor in widening the knowledge gap. And it is this precious commodity—time—that will once again tip the balance in favor of students from Chestnut Hill compared to their counterparts in the Badlands, upending the fragile level playing field and the development of information capital.

IF YOU WOULD ASK an outside auditor to review the digital resources of Chestnut Hill and Lillian Marrero libraries, he or she would likely report that they are comparable. Statistics would undoubtedly show that these libraries include equal numbers of computers along with Internet access, not to mention the equal numbers of human resources—librarians, technology assistants, and volunteers—willing to help the young novice and interested patron. In fact, you could even argue that the Lillian Marrero library has a unique advantage, having received a special gift of Gateway computers to provide special classes for adults on computers. Conduct a similar audit in the public schools, and you would find a similar picture: resources equal if not better due to special grants in schools in the low-income areas compared to middle- and upper-income neighborhoods. In short, confirming data from the National Center for Education Statistics (2000), the digital divide has closed.

Nevertheless, these statistics overlook a critical feature: most students hone their digital skills in their home, not in libraries or schools. And here statistics vary dramatically. Fewer than a third of the families living in the Badlands own even a working computer; Internet access is rare. For example, in Chestnut Hill, you will find three computer shops all within a stone's throw of Main Street, along with a computer "spa," the local repair shop, in case you get in trouble. Although firm statistics are hard to come by, local principals indicate that there are more laptops per home in Chestnut Hill than television sets. By contrast, the Badlands has neither computer stores nor repair shops anywhere in close proximity.

Now the reason this matters is that in places like the Badlands, it puts pressure on the public resources to fill in the gap. Students will need to rely on school resources when school is in session and the libraries when it is not. Students from Chestnut Hill, on the other hand, can work at home. In other words, the digital divide is still there; it's just taken a different form.

Take the average day at Lillian Marrero library, and here is what you are likely to see. At 2:45 p.m. in the afternoon, the onrush begins, with about 30 or so students signing in to get a "30-minute slot" on the computer. This means that sometimes a student's reservation might be several hours away. With no other resources available, he may leave the library until his time

The Old and New Literacies

slot comes up. Analogous to a restaurant reservation, however, if he is late or a no-show he will have to go to the end of the line and start the process all over again.

Now the system gets even more complicated. For example, on this particular day at the library, six computer stations are occupied: three people are working independently; another man is working with his young son, and two pairs of boys are working together. Two computers are vacant due to no-shows. If someone steps in to take the no-show's place, he or she must forfeit the scheduled time for later that day. This creates two risks for the potential taker: you can end up with less than your full 30-minute slot; or you can lose out altogether if the no-show arrives after you have forfeited your other time. Finally, since a 30-minute time slot is often not sufficient to finish an assignment, you will have to start the sign-up process all over again, being mindful that the library closes at 6:00 p.m.

Obviously, this is neither the fault of the library nor their need to enforce certain policies. Rather, these problems result from undue pressure on limited public resources. To give you an example, we scout other public programs for computers and Internet access for students in the Badlands neighborhood. We visit recreation centers, after-school programs, and boys' and girls' clubs throughout the neighborhood. In Table 6.1, you can get a sense of the dearth of resources available to students. In fact, it makes the library look like a treasure trove of Internet access.

Table 6.1. Programs That Provide Access to Computers in the Philadelphia Badlands

Total number of Computers (after-school programs, community centers, libraries)	17 programs 128 computers
Total number of children ages 5–18 living in area (U.S. Census Data)	7,729
Average computers available per child in zip code	About 2 for every 100 children
Computers per child registered in programs with no time limits (i.e., no scheduled computer time/program does not monitor use)	.30
Computers per child registered in programs with time limits (i.e., scheduled computer time/program monitors use)	.58
Average daily use per child in programs with scheduled computer time	32.2 minutes/day

For instance, we count 17 programs for these 7,729 students in the Badlands, for a total of 128 computers across all programs. This amounts to about 2 computers for every 100 children. These numbers are overestimates actually, for many of the computers are old, broken, and missing letters on their keyboards, with only intermittent Internet access. When the Internet is available, filters prevent students from easy navigation.

Time slots in these programs are even stricter than the library. There are often 30 to 75 children waiting for a 30-minute time slot. When they do get access, most of the activities are related enrichment activities, games, and other projects. Even when they have Internet access, with no internal filters, there is concern about downloading inappropriate content. With few adults available for supervision, one director reports that it is easier and safer to work on arts projects or dance classes than on computer-related activities. Further, none of these programs stay open past 6:00 p.m.

In short, one could reasonably argue that if time is our denominator, and if these patterns are endemic to neighborhoods like the Badlands and Chestnut Hill, the digital divide has increased substantially in recent years. With personal computers and laptops at their disposal in their homes, students from Chestnut Hill are likely to have the time to master the technical aspects and applications with facility, while students from the Badlands will only have available short bursts of time to engage in any activity.

Table 6.2. Sample Programs That Provide Access to Computers in the Badlands

After-School Program	# of Computers/ # of Children	Time	Uses	Internet
Dept. of Recreation	2/50	Daily 30 minutes	Recreation/ Some research with CDs	No
Elementary School Program	0/60			Send students to library
Salvation Army	6/35–70 Students	1 x per week for 30 minutes	Enrichment/ recreation	Yes, with filters
Taller Puertoriqueno	3/20–75 Students	Occasionally	Homework	No

WITH LITTLE TIME to develop skills, this is what we find at Lillian Marrero library. It is 5:15 p.m., 45 minutes before the library is set to close. Two middle-school girls, Angelica and Genesis, are sitting side by side patiently waiting for their turn at the computers. They are here to work on an assignment for Black History month, due 2 days from now. Their teacher has directed the students to google the term "African American educators," and "a whole bunch of names will come up." They are to pick three educators, gather biographical information about them, and write a report. Interestingly, notice the language that the teacher uses and the assumptions that are implicit in these statements. It is assumed, for example, that a student knows how to search for information, critically examine its content, synthesize materials from a veritable flood of information, and put all this together in a coherent report. Here is what actually happens.

By the time the girls' turn comes up at the computer stations, it is now 5:25 p.m., giving them 20 or so minutes to do their work. Knowing that time is short, the LEAP leader comes over to help guide them. "As quickly as you can, type in 'African American educators,'" she says to them. "How do you spell *educators*?" Angelica asks. The LEAP leader spells the word, and guides her to a link for Mary Macleod Bethune, and directs Angelica to open it. They each read the page silently. "So do you think she's an educator? Angelica nods her head, and pulls out her notebook to start copying, word for word, what is on the website. She tells the LEAP leader that she also needs a printout of Bethune's photograph.

Directing her with the mouse, the LEAP leader points to the top center of the screen, and says "Go to Google images and type her [Bethune's] name. Put a space after each word. Then click images. Then click image search." Angelica moves the mouse to click on something and the LEAP leader quickly intercedes, "That's a commercial, so no!!" A page of images comes up and Angelica points to the photograph of Bethune that she wants.

The time is getting short, and the LEAP leader asks, "Do you know how to select something and copy it?" Angelica shakes her head. Step by step, she directs Angelica, "Go back. Click 'view image.' Now right-click the mouse." Angelica does not have the cursor directly over the image, so it doesn't work. "Move it up. Just a bit more. Now click. Go to copy. Now open Microsoft Office Word. Now paste." Throughout the process, Angelica struggles, left, then right, clicking at images. Soon, the leader takes over the mouse to finish the print request. It is now 5:42 p.m.

At the same time following Angelica's lead, Genesis has also typed "African American educators," and while the LEAP leader is now running off to retrieve the image, the Word document that Genesis has been typing from is long gone from the computer screen. "Did you close it?" the leader asks. Genesis looks up and nods her head. "Oh shoot!" she responds, and with one minute left, she says, "You go ahead and keep doing what you're doing. I'm going to find that picture again and I'll print it out. " Commandeering the mouse, after a few clicks she says, "Okay, here it is" as the printer spits out the page.

Meanwhile the girls are stacking up their belongings. On top of Angelica's folder and notebook, ready for checkout is the video *Saw II,* a horror movie with an R rating for "grisly violence and gore, terror, language, and drug content." Looking her straight in the eye, the LEAP leader says, "Here, I'll trade you," giving her the picture of Bethune as Angelica reluctantly hands over the video. The girls slip on their jackets and head out.

Communication scholars might place this scene in the late 1990s—maybe even earlier—when it was common for computers to freeze, and for search engines to go unfriendly. However it actually occurred in 2009, when the term "to google" had become common parlance. With limited time available to develop the conscious strategic processes of information navigation, these students have not had the experiences and opportunities to access complex content. Under these conditions, such assignments can become extremely grueling exercises, leading students to emphasize "getting the work done" rather than learning from it.

THE INTERNET MAY HAVE fundamentally changed how we read, write, and gather information. Nevertheless, these new skills are actually built on some foundational "old" literacy skills—the ability to decode and comprehend text. Although the stunted language teenagers might use to tap out text and instant messages like "C U 2nite" might work for social networking, you won't get far on an Internet search with this type of writing. In fact, you could argue that basic literacy skills are even more essential than ever, serving as the entry point for the kinds of sophisticated skills that students will need to use media and complex information systems. For example, consider Angelica's dilemma as she tries to learn more about African American educators. To navigate, she needs to know how to spell *educator*. If she spells it like *educaters*, Google or some other search engine will likely pop up with the statement "Do you mean 'educators'?" But if she spells, it like "edukators," what will turn up is a movie in which three activists are organizing a kidnapping plot. In other words, there are spelling miscues, and then there are spelling disasters.

Unlike school texts, texts online are not carefully calibrated to readability levels. Vocabulary, concepts, and content may be dense, and sentences long and complicated. Words can take on specialized meanings (e.g., *operation* has a very different meaning in mathematics than in day-to-day discourse). Increasingly, therefore, students like Angelica and Genesis will have to rely on self-teaching strategies to read and learn online.

Self-teaching, in this context, works like this: In order to benefit from the massive influx of words coming at them on the Internet—academic words with complex concepts—students will need to know about 90–95% of words in order to get their basic meaning. This is the percentage that will allow readers to get the main thrust of what is written. The other 5% of the words will likely be guessed at, based on the context of what he or she is reading. None of these guesses will be totally accurate, but with repeated encounters with words, students will accumulate more and more information until they have a pretty good notion of what the word means. The benefit is that with 90–95% of the words known, they'll learn the other 5–10% through incidental exposure. This is how most of us read informational text online, as well as newspapers and magazines, and continue to enrich our vocabulary.

Now take a somewhat different example. What if students don't know at least 90% of the words in a text? What if the percentage is more like 75%, with the knowledge of only three out of four words? Studies show that students will be frustrated and will have difficulty getting through the text on the screen. In this respect, they will experience a double dose of disadvantage: They will miss out on information from the text, and they will not learn many new words.

Getting the meanings of words in these complex contexts, however, is only a precondition of comprehending materials online. The second part is world knowledge. In other words, to make use of the words you are reading, you will also need a threshold of knowledge about a topic. For example, googling the word *democracy,* a common study assignment for students in high school, you find this description on Wikipedia:

> **Democracy** is a form of government in which all citizens have
> an equal say in the decisions that affect their lives. Ideally, this
> includes equal (and more or less direct) participation in the proposal,
> development and passage of legislation into law. It can also encompass
> social, economic and cultural conditions that enable the free and equal
> practice of political self-determination. The term comes from the
> Greek: δημοκρατία—(*dêmokratía*) "rule of the people", which was coined
> from δῆμος (*dêmos*) "people" and κράτος (*Kratos*) "power," in the middle
> of the 5th–4th century B.C. to denote the political systems then existing
> in some Greek city-states, notably Athens following a popular uprising
> in 508 B.C.

Although the average high school student might be able to understand the words "political determination" and "passage of legislation into law," you could spend a full semester on just one of these terms. Consequently, this is when self-teaching gets hard. Unlike word knowledge, where you can come up with a good guess based on the context of what you are reading, you need background knowledge to understand this definition and the concepts that lie behind it. However, not implicit like word learning, world knowledge is best learned when some knowledgeable other—a more capable peer, a parent, a teacher can assist and provide some important background information. Moreover, world knowledge is not stochastic. It's hard to pick up random facts and store them in long-term memory. According to cognitive psychologists, knowledge builds on prior knowledge, structured in a way that enables students to access it easily.

What this means is that reading online requires good, solid, old-fashioned literacy skills—decoding, vocabulary, and background knowledge to comprehend content—in addition to the new literacy skills. For students who have these foundational skills, mastering the technical aspects of these ever-evolving media tools may seem increasingly second nature, adding little cognitive demand to how they may normally read. Zigzagging through a cornucopia of words, pictures, video, and sounds, locating information quickly and accurately, and corroborating findings on multiple sites, may no sooner constitute "new" literacy practices than the typewriter once did for writing composition. Experienced users may be able read five websites, an op-ed article, and a blog post or two in a tenth of the time it would normally take to read a 400-page text.

Armed with their personal laptops, this is the type of skill level we see among students at the Chestnut Hill library. For example, one of our teenage interviewees, Zachary, often stays awake until 2:00 or 3:00 in the morning reading articles about technology and politics–his current passions–on up to 100 different websites. He says, "On the Internet you can hear from a bunch of people. They may not be pedigreed professors. They may be someone in a shed working on a conspiracy theory." Though he also loves to read books, Zachary craves the interaction with people all across the country, spending long stretches of time in his room on the web. He's not the only one. Informal interviews with his friends at the library tell us that on a typical day, they will spend over 2 hours online, more than double the figures reported by the Kaiser Family Foundation survey (Rideout, Foehr, & Roberts, 2010).

The kinds of skills that Zachary and his friends have developed–navigating quickly and accurately to multiple sites, engaging with others in virtual worlds–come about only after many hours of use. Reading online is part of their lives. It is a new form of play. We watch as they engage in this type of literacy-based play at the Chestnut Hill library, about 15 minutes after school has let out.

Already several students are clustered around the computer, checking the Google map and showing each other satellite views of their school locations. Within moments, one of the friends trots over to the computer and commandeers the mouse. A pop-up ad covers the middle of the screen. He clicks on it. Suddenly a new larger window with several thumbnail pictures opens up, covering most of the map. It is the bare buttocks of a woman. Immediately a large throng of teens hunker around the computer. Flustered, the first boy looks up to see if anyone has noticed. Eyeing us, he blushes and moves away from the computer screen while another quickly maneuvers the mouse and makes the images go away. Before anyone can see, with a few more clicks of the mouse, they open a website with pictures from the school the boys attend. This catches the attention of two more boys. Together, they scan the array of photographs, alternatively clicking on one to enlarge it and studying it. Spontaneously, they begin to work on what looks like a web-based scrapbook of pictures and events in school, moving from site to site, playing out their work to an ever-widening audience of students, all wanting to contribute. Meanwhile, some students click their way to a site called ThisIBelieve.org, a collection of personal essays, to see if any might work, and then navigate to their own class website, where they read and critique their own essays.

The differences in their facility to maneuver the web and its resources are immediately apparent in these activities: these students know where to go on the Internet, how to synthesize disparate sources of information and integrate it, all in rapid-fire strategic movements. It's like they have traded in their pencils for a keyboard, so innate are their actions. And their facility, gamesmanship, and playfulness comes about in part by having the time and access to these digital tools, all of which have been denied to students at Lillian Marrero.

EVEN THE LIBRARY, the hallmark of educational equity in our country, therefore, cannot counter the less visible inequity of time distribution for students across these two communities. Examining teenagers' computer use in our last year of data collection in 2010, we took an average week and calculated over 40 hours of activity, the time per application, purpose, amount of reading, and the degree of challenge in reading. Our numbers, shown in Table 6.3, are striking.

First, note that the average amount of time spent on the computer is longer for students at Chestnut Hill than at Lillian Marrero. Although this might appear paradoxical at first, the reason becomes plain after hours of observations: given that most students own a laptop, fewer students sign up for the computer at Chestnut Hill. At times, the librarians do not even observe the 30-minute time restrictions since there are no waiting lines or long sign-up lists. At Lillian Marrero, on the other hand, students actually receive less than their 30-minute allotment, once again due to the enormous backlog of people grabbing time slots from those who might not show up on time. And when your time is limited, with others waiting for their turns, this is what you are likely to see:

3:30: Goes to Google. Types Civil War. Does not get desired results.
3:31: Types in other websites; dates, people connected with the Civil War. Does not seem to get the website he wants. Does not ask for help.

Table 6.3. Students Computer Use in Libraries

	Chestnut Hill	**Lillian Marrero**
Hours of Computer use observed	20	20
Total minutes observed	1,210	1,241
Average time spent on computer	28 minutes	18 minutes
Number of lines of print read per student	11	3.9
Challenge Level		
Below reading level	10%	53%
At reading level	85%	47%
Above reading level	5%	0%

3:40: Not happy with web searches. Types in website: bonustv.com

3:42: Back to Google. Types in brideofchucky.com (horror movie). Watches movie.

3:50: Tech assistant tells him his time is up.

In contrast, this is what we see for a student at Chestnut Hill:

3:15: Teenager sits down at the computer and immediately clicks on Encarta Encyclopedia. Types in "Winston Churchill." Gets article with pictures, various battle campaigns in World War II. He reads through it, looking for certain things that he checks off against a list from school. Goes to another website on the same topic, reads through the article, looking for specific things requested on the list. He checks out a bunch more websites; looks at Google images, downloads a picture or two, and prints them out.

3:47: Grabs his things and leaves. No one has disturbed him throughout his work. No one has asked him to leave the computer.

Second, you can see how these time differentials make a difference with regard to what kinds of activities students are likely to engage in when you might think you have a very tight timeline versus when time is not a concern. In the case of students from Lillian Marrero, we find that the games and movies and online TV programs also have costs on the amount of reading they are likely to do. Over the hours we observed, students at Chestnut Hill are likely to read 11 lines of print, compared to 3.9 lines of print for students at Lillian Marrero. And third, once again, the challenge level of these materials is strikingly different. Similar to a pattern we noted many years before, students at Lillian Marrero are reading below level, indicative of using the computer more for entertainment-like activities than learning. When time becomes such a precious commodity, it may become difficult for a teen to rationalize spending time reading about Winston Churchill when he or she can more easily download a horror movie.

It might appear, then, that the digital divide is closing, and that all students are regularly spending hours in front of the computer. Many are. But they are living in areas like Chestnut Hill where, at a moment's notice, they can check their email; or peruse myyearbook.com, a social networking site, reading messages or posting updates on their moods and latest activities; or visit fanfiction.net, reading and commenting on stories written by users based on books, television shows, or movies. These students are not living in places like the Philadelphia Badlands, with limited to no access to the Internet, and where all the fail-safe programs that might provide it close down at 6:00 p.m.

Our failure to examine the potential of the Internet for closing the knowledge gap, and increasing opportunities for information capital, was stymied by this factor of time. However, we can elicit two crucial messages from our analysis. If such time differentials continue unabated, the knowledge gap will increase substantially, further accentuating inequality across class lines. Further, it becomes doubly imperative for precisely those students whose abilities are most in need of bolstering to have greater access to these resources, for it is the very act of reading and using these new literacies that can build their capacities.

CHAPTER 7

Developing
Information Capital

Throughout most of our history, technological innovation involved machines replacing humans in performing physical or monotonous tasks. Robots took over the heavy lifting jobs in factories and the typewriter facilitated the arduous task of the scribe. But today's computer age is replacing humans in more fundamental ways. Computerization now has the advantage over humans in carrying out basic information-processing tasks with great speed and accuracy. Increasingly, what we are seeing is a major conversion in the kinds of information processing that are valued and unique to human endeavors–the importance of expert thinking. Here is the human advantage.

Once we were a culture that prized the generalist–the jack-of-all-trades. Today, we are a culture of the specialist, the expert in a particular domain (Jones, 2009). Knowledge has power and is seen as an essential component of human capital. Unlike the generalist, the expert is someone with deep knowledge of a topic. The expert is the person who not only knows everything about a game but who can anticipate the next play. These types of experts have knowledge at their fingertips, organized in ways that facilitate effective problem-solving. They're able to quickly recognize large chunks of information, see the deep features of a problem, and come up with new solutions. They can judge when something isn't working, and are facile enough to figure out a new strategy. In short, they learn faster and think smarter.

A growing number of educators, business leaders, and politicians describe these abilities as 21st-century skills (Rotherham & Willingham, 2009). In addition to new literacies, there are the Four C's that students will need to compete in the global society: critical thinking, communication, collaboration, and creativity. It's exciting to believe that we live in times so revolutionary that they demand higher-level skills. But in fact, the need for mastery of higher-level thinking ranging from facts to complex thinking has always been central to human progress. What's actually new is the extent to which individual success and the quality of our economy now demands such skills. It is the value-added feature in any successful enterprise, the competitive edge that defines the difference between those who are merely knowledge workers and those who are knowledge creators.

These skills involve logical, analytical thinking that often goes beyond what the situation calls for. It is not just about using knowledge or applying it to a problem; rather, this type of expertise involves knowledge development. To succeed in an Algebra class, for example, a student must have achieved the instructional goals implicit in the course and have at least memorized certain routines and successfully applied these to a number of unique problems. To be on track for becoming a mathematician, an expert in the field, it is obviously necessary to have a similar foundation but also to pursue knowledge-building goals–goals that extend beyond the immediate to constructing new mathematical knowledge in one's own way and following its implications. It is the production of new knowledge, an act of creativity as if it were an artistic conception that is the key to the development of information capital.

In this chapter, we examine this last phase of our theory of action. For this type of information capital to develop, students will not only need access to resources and time to pursue their interests, but opportunity to engage in communities of practice with colleagues and mentors that support these endeavors. In the previous chapters, we have documented how the disparities in access to resources and time differentials relate to the development of reading and new literacy skills critical for rapidly acquiring knowledge. In this chapter we will first describe how this drive for expertise, inherent in this second mode of information capital, develops early on in children's lives. We will then see how opportunities to build on one's knowledge assets through communities of practice differ in neighborhoods of poverty and privilege, affecting the development of a learning ecology that prizes expertise.

IT WASN'T UNTIL OUR FINAL YEARS of data collection that we learned about the power of developing expertise in the formation of information capital. Before that, our theory of action was more linear and conventional; in other words, we believed that if students could develop basic literacy skills–decoding and comprehension skills, in particular–they would be likely to make the critical transition from learning to read to reading to learn. From here, we assumed that with the prodigious amount of information flowing from the Internet, there lay the potential to increase reading volume, developing skills and a host of different knowledge bases. Nevertheless, our theory of action never spoke to the purposes for independent reading, or what drives people to seek information in the first place. Now, as we watched students' activities in the libraries, we began to understand their motivational intent. It is in the pursuit of expertise.

Interestingly, when scientists first began to study expertise, they assumed that experts must be smarter or more talented than novices (Nisbett, 2009). They studied experts in all sorts of fields–puzzle solvers, chess masters, violinists, and even race track betters. These scientists quickly learned that the key difference between experts and novices was not mental power. It was knowledge power. However, it was not just the cumulative product of factual knowledge. Rather, it was the conceptual, analytic, deep understanding of a particular domain, organized in particular ways, that made knowledge more accessible, functional, and efficient (Chi & Ceci, 1987; Glaser, 1984). For example, the chess expert looking at a board doesn't see 16 white pieces—he sees several clusters of pieces, with each cluster defined by the relationship of the pieces to one another and to opposing pieces. In other words, for experts, the compacting of information into a larger conceptual picture allows the expert to circumvent the limitations of working memory, enabling them to more quickly retrieve information, analyze the situation, and apply potential solutions.

Experts also have considerable procedural knowledge. They internalize the routines to get something done. Generally, this type of knowledge develops slowly at first. Even Sherlock Holmes's performance in solving a case would be characterized as slow, effortful, and error prone, at least at the outset. As an expert, he reflects on the nature of the problem and considers his clues from different perspectives. From the outside, it will appear as if he is doing nothing and not making much progress. But once he understands the problem, he solves it better and faster than any of his peers.

This ability to gather the whole picture and figure out what steps to take to solve problems actually comes from practice. K. Anders Ericsson (Ericsson, Krampe, & Tesch-Romer, 1993) describes it as "deliberate practice," the kind of repeated effort designed to improve accuracy and speed of performance. It's not short-lived or simple. It often extends over a period of 10 or so years. Over time, people build a mental model that forms the framework for greater knowledge. It helps you distinguish relevant from irrelevant information, predict what comes next, and gives you a superior structure for remembering things.

Given that children start out as universal novices, how does expertise develop? Generally it starts out early on as children engage in playful activity. Consider Benjamin, a 3-year-old who sees dolphins for the first time in the ocean. He is fascinated, and asks lots of questions about them. His parents respond to his interest, and during their next visit to the library, they take out several books on whales and dolphins. He likes these books a lot and asks his parents to read them again and again. Maybe his father takes a look at the Discovery channel and finds a program on oceanography. They watch and talk about it together. As Benjamin's knowledge about these mammals deepens, the family checks out more advanced books on the topic. They look for posters, with vital statistics about the animals, and take trips to conservation sites to learn how to protect the animals from harm. Soon Benjamin is known in his preschool as an "orca whale" specialist, an expert who knows a lot of domain-specific knowledge, and the go-to person when there are questions that come up about these fascinating animals. His knowledge of the words and the world about whales is numerous, well-organized, and flexible. He has become a young expert in a domain.

ACQUIRING EXPERTISE requires learning the explicit knowledge of a field, the practices of its community, and the interplay between the two. In the past, we used to think of this type of deep knowledge, both its tacit and explicit dimensions, as residing in the individual mind. More recently, we have come to recognize that it also requires immersion in a community of practice, enculturation in its ways of seeing, interpreting, and acting. Much of the know-how or knowing comes about through participating with others who are likewise engaged in collaborative activity (Brown, Collins, & Duguid, 1989). For example, over the last 5 decades, there has been a dramatic shift from the individual working as solo author in the production of knowledge to a teamwork model. Analyzing over 21 million scientific papers and patents in the Institute for Scientific Information databases and an additional 2.1 million patent records, Stefan Wuchty and his colleagues (Wuchty, Jones, & Uzzi, 1997) found that patents in science, technology, engineering—innovations that have changed our lives—are increasingly produced by teams. It's the coordination of teams of experts—people who are deeply knowledgeable in a specialization working alongside others with complementary skills—that accounts for growth in our nation's and the world's economy. It's like a puzzle, where different specializations fit together to form a coherent, high-impact picture.

Consequently, the Internet offers the potential to create a new learning ecology that supports the development of information capital. It can create a virtual collection of communities of practice. Further, it can involve a dynamic and interdependent community of experts that can build on one another's knowledge assets, creating larger networks with a greater number of people. In fact, one of the things that makes such a learning ecology so powerful and adaptive is its diversity of knowledge assets. You can literally have young Benjamin participating in an interest group conversation about orca whales with university experts across the country.

Nevertheless, although the virtual capabilities of the web are endless, communities of practice often get started through informal, face-to-face connections, such as students with common interests who frequent the same hangouts. For example, the Silicon Valley phenomenon began as students worked on projects in university coursework; many of them, then, got part-time jobs in surrounding firms, new firms spun out of the universities, employees were retrained on campus, and larger communities of practice became dependent on the expertise of one another (Brown, 2000). The web, of course, significantly augments and cements these relationships, building a rich fabric that combines the efforts of many, increasing the intellectual density of cross-linkages. At the same time, however, there is no substitute for the personal interactions and peer-to-peer group activities in establishing communities of practice.

Therefore, in our final year of data collection, our goal was to examine how the Internet might contribute to developing expertise and communities of practice in our two neighborhoods. Although both time and opportunity to use the Internet was at a premium in the library for students in the Badlands during the year, we reasoned the summer, with its more open-ended schedule, might provide a more optimal time for watching students in both communities pursue their interests and expertise. We also knew that the summer months traditionally are among the most pernicious causes for exacerbating the achievement gap. In Barbara Heyns' classic study (1978), for example, she found that poor children were most dependent on schooling to increase achievement; without school, their rates of growth were slowed or reversed. In contrast, well-to-do children were capable of augmenting their achievement whether or not schools were open, at rates approximating those found in school. If the Internet attraction in the libraries could help level the playing field at least to some degree, we could potentially see a learning loss transform into a learning gain.

However, what Heyns could not have possibly forecasted in her 1978 book—nor did we in 2010—was the extent to which summer programs have evolved over the years. It used to be that the idyllic summer included some time off from schedules, fun and freedom at the beach, a week or two away at sleep-over camp. Now for students like those in Chestnut Hill, summers aren't just about hanging out at the library. Instead, they've taken on a new dimension and specialization, giving students time to develop their expertise in communities of practice.

AT FIRST, we were perplexed by the absence of the usual cacophony of teens huddling around the computers in the afternoons at the Chestnut Hill library. We subsequently learned, however, that summers in this neighborhood are heavily scheduled, with many attending specialized camps in the area. Among the more popular, especially with teens, are computer-related day camps, which we decided to visit on several occasions.

The Digital Media summer camp is such a camp, located on a sweeping, farm-like swath of land at Temple University's Ambler campus close by in Montgomery County. The site of the university's horticultural programs, the grounds' abundant trees, shrubs, and flowers almost dwarf the many converted houses and low-slung buildings. We meander through the lush campus, past the barn and silo and eventually wind our way to the newest building on campus, the Learning Center. Built to house undergraduate and graduate classes, this gleaming, modern, two-story structure is the epitome of new: new furniture, windows, desks, and 20–25 computer workstations.

The Advanced Digital Photography class is a 4-week program designed to help students, ages 12–17, become more expert in the use of these media tools. Run by a commercial photographer in Philadelphia, the class of eight is meeting for a lively debate about the merits of two different designs developed by one of the students. Huddling together over the circuit diagrams, the students are analyzing possible faults, discussing issues of design, proposing alternatives, teasing out one another's assumptions, and making the case for their point of view.

They are uploading and exporting to one another's computers, when one of the 12-year-olds decides to take a different picture of his friend to upload. He focuses on his friend, and after a good 5 seconds the camera flashes. "Wait a second," his friend asks, "what's wrong with that camera? Why did it take so long to take a picture–something must be wrong." No, no, the boy protests, "There's nothing wrong; it's just waiting for the smile, and then it flashes." An older boy answers, "That's not a smile, that's a histograph. The histograph is telling you about the exposure; the left side shows the darkest areas of the picture, and the right side the brightest."Another joins in to tell him, "Remember, you can't always tell by looking in the viewfinder how your picture will turn out. The camera often lies. The pictures look good in the viewfinder but you don't know if you have a good exposure. And you really can't tell the exposure until you look at the histograph." Still another asks, "But can it tell you about the contrast?" Terrance pipes in, "This is the way I do it. You can tell through the graph how much information your camera has captured."

The conversations seem focused on solving problems, sharing opinions, and trying new ideas without repercussions. As we watch students upload their pictures with their iMacs and use Photoshop, card readers, imports, contrasts, and histographs, it is evident that the students are becoming both fluent and capable with the camera equipment and the computers. The familiarity of these activities seems to create a comfort level that invites candid discussions. Students ask questions, think critically, and adjust their conceptions–more or less learning as they go. Throughout the activities, the teacher (or camp counselor) seems to stay somewhat in the background, there to answer questions, but at the same time encouraging students to work together to solve problems. For example, we see how common misconceptions–such as a boy who thought the "smile" was driving the camera rather than the exposure, or the boy who asked about the contrast–are resolved through clarifying questions, synthesizing information from different experiences as they try to come up with solutions.

It is like watching expertise develop in action. Much of the knowledge is brought forth in action through participation with people, around real problems. Knowledge is put into action—performance gets better initially. Knowledge then goes deeper; performance begins to pick up speed again, and gets better with deliberate practice. As students accumulate knowledge, they develop a set of specific routines or procedures, which become automatic over time. This mechanism shows how the expert's cognitive processing is really different from that of a novice. The novice relies on the interpretation and retrieval of information from long-term to short-term memory. Instead, the expert relies on a large set of procedural rules, the context-specific representation of a skill that can be quickly and efficiently executed. Learning *and* doing, not learning *by* doing, is the road to expertise for these students at summer camp.

THE DIGITAL ACADEMY IS JUST one of the camps around the Chestnut Hill area we visited over the summer. We will come to see programs in digital film-making, robotics, web design, video design, and others. Developing expertise in these areas is very specific, and students select their specialty carefully. Expertise in video-game design, it turns out, has little transfer to proficiency in another domain, like robotics. Within a specific domain, however, there is transfer from one task to another. For example, the extent to which a person has learned about programming robots to perform certain functions may transfer to another more complex application in robotics. This is what we see when we enter Dr. Silage's advanced robotics summer program, the third in a series of robotics classes for these students ranging in age from 11 to 15 years old: engineering in a whole new dimension.

Students are so engaged in building robots that they hardly notice the new visitors in the room. They're using LEGOXT, a fairly complicated engineering program despite the Lego name. We first see a demonstration by Dr. Silage, in which he uses familiar words in ways we've never heard of: "Slave 1 reports to the Master. It's usually something like ACK1." He then goes on to talk about "the necessary variables that we need to keep things moving from distance A to distance B." Before each student is a box full of Legos, which some have already constructed in what look like robot cars.

Although we may be totally lost in this conversation, the students are not. After the discussion on the board, the group is very quiet as they turn to the computer program which is very complicated with diagrams, schematics, and math formulas. It turns out that they are designing the robot cars to do extraordinary things. "Some of these kids are doing amazing things," says Dr. Silage. "Martin, here, only eleven, has just created a reaction time tester. It's an instrument that is designed to go on jet control panels. It tests how alert the pilots are. He designed it on his own."

**Engaging in
Communities
of Practice**

Once again, we watch the rich interplay between knowledge and practice. As developmental psychologist Jerome Bruner brilliantly observed (Bruner, 1977; Bruner, Goodnow, & Austin, 1956), we can teach people *about* a subject matter like engineering–its concepts, conceptual frameworks, its facts–and provide them with explicit knowledge of the field. But *being* an engineer involves a lot more than getting all the answers right on the test. To be an engineer, students must also learn the practices of the field, the procedural knowledge in the community of engineers that has to do with things like what constitutes an interesting question, what design may be good enough *or* even elegant. Learning to be an engineer (as opposed to learning about engineering) is more than just having domain-specific knowledge, but also the ability to acquire the demanding practices of its community. And for 40 intensive hours, these students will practice what it is like to be an engineer, developing their expertise in a community of practice.

As we watch these students working so intently and collaboratively on these complicated machines, it becomes evident how much more they can know through participation with other people–around real problems. The problem-solving conversations that we overhear might remind someone of a community of designers who get together for a lively debate about the merits of different designs, dueling over cutting-edge ideas. You hear them discuss knotty problems, probe one another's ideas, and gently offer suggestions. What appears to make them so successful is their ability to generate excitement and relevance, with each member contributing to the solution. Although many factors are in place here, nothing seems to substitute for the sense of "aliveness" in the learning process.

The Internet is part of the learning ecology throughout all of these activities. Students use the web constantly for information. It becomes part of the constellation of tools, a means to build knowledge. In this respect, it serves students' purposes, extending the reach of their interactions beyond their immediate geographic limitations. It increases the flow of information, but does not obviate the need for community. In fact, it expands the possibilities for community and calls for a greater diversity of talents and expertise based on shared practice.

IT'S NOT ABOUT SUMMER GAIN in the Philadelphia Badlands. It's about summer loss and how to redeem the summer as an educational resource. Consequently, the strains on the library for time and resources only quadruple during the summer months for a host of reasons: air-conditioning is a rare commodity in this part of town, drawing hundreds of people to the library; the instability of child care for working parents makes the library a destination home for young children who spend much of their day there; and as a public resource, summer camps "camp out" at the library, booking hour after hour of story time, club activities, and computer sessions. Access and time to use the Internet, we come to learn, is even more precious in the summer than during the school year.

On this side of town the Digital Media Academy-type programs are replaced by the Salvation Army or others, designed to provide students with "a safe and supportive environment" or to "prevent drug abuse" or "get kids off the street." Regardless of the differences in their names or missions, these programs are for students, ages 8–14, who might otherwise languish on street corners or in front of glowing screens for days on end. The strategy is to build on the city's existing patchwork of day camps, community centers, and special programs while keeping the costs low.

The programs try to take advantage of resources like the library throughout the city, and so we meet Erin, head of the summer reading program at Lillian Marrero. Erin's job is to register students for the summer reading program at the library. The program is designed to encourage students to read as many books as possible to prevent the loss of reading skills over the summer. Students are given a workbook and awarded stickers for each book title they read and write down in their workbook. Prizes are given for their efforts. This week's prizes are pencils and small, plastic wild animal figures.

The weekly raffle is another component of the program. Students win additional prizes if they answer a question about the book they have read. Slips with the questions and answers are posted around the summer reading program desk. Two award winners look like this:

> Question: What happens to the character in the story?
> Answer: She died.
> Question: Did this book make you angry? Or laugh? Or cry? Which and why?
> Answer: Cry. When he fell.

On the day we visit, four camp counselors from the Timothy Academy, along with 32 children, are participating in the summer reading program. Children seem to be acting more like they are in a candy shop than a library, and soon there is complete bedlam. By the time the counselors get the group together and distribute the right summer reading folder to the right child, there are 15 minutes left. One at a time, children are allowed to go to the stacks, grab a book, write down the title, and if they are inclined, write about the book in one phrase (or less). Fewer than half of the students get a turn before it is time to leave. Within this time frame, we did not see any reading at all.

As head of the program, Erin will repeat this task—giving out workbooks, stickers, plastic figures—and getting the folders back, four or five times per day. Although she finds the activities a bit tedious, the program fits well with her summer schedule. She has had the job for the last 2 years, and doesn't mind interacting with the kids, though she admits that "I'd never want to be a teacher." She knows the kids make lots of mistakes when they write, but hasn't had the time to help them correct their work.

If the crowds of students at the library seem overwhelming in the winter, it can look like Macy's on the day after Thanksgiving in the summer. The library is a stop on the camp and community program tour. Tim, a youth advocate camp counselor, responsible for supervising, mentoring, and encouraging adolescents who are "in trouble," comes here at least once a week. "I pick a book and give them a list of questions to answer. I try to keep their minds fresh during the summer. Inner-city kids don't read. They just don't see the importance of it. I try to get them to see the value of reading." Asked what other things they do here, Tim adds, "We use the computer. I let them go and browse the Internet for a few minutes. Sometimes I give them a topic to look up and we work on getting them to do that. If I didn't get them on the computer, they would never get on one."

The program is part of a teen camp run by the city for at-risk or troubled youth. During the school year, Tim makes sure the students get to school and spends their after-school time with them. In the summer, the kids spend part of their day in this structured program. Tim goes on, "The boys have done some neat things. They went to the Franklin Institute this week. We took the Big Bus Sightseeing tour. They like that because they could ride up top. Yesterday we did a tour of City Hall."

We ask Tim about their future. He shakes his head. "I try my best to get them thinking about getting jobs. I brought them a Rite Aid application. Some tried to fill it out and got some of it right. Some can't read and won't even participate."

Throughout our conversation, we are struck by Tim's weariness. He is tired. Having worked at the job for over 5 years, the advocate part of his responsibilities seems to have vanished or gone deep underground. The dreams and hopes he might have had for these students have turned into clichéd stereotypes: "These kids have a microwave mentality. They want something now. They don't want to work and get it." A bit later, he says, "School is not important for these kids. And it is getting worse. Five years ago, the kids would complain about going to school, but they knew they had to go. These kids that I have now just say 'I'm just not going to school. I just don't want to achieve.'"

It would be challenging to find a better example of the "self-fulfilling prophecy," the psychological axiom that explains how negative thoughts create reality. Coined by the sociologist Robert Merton (1948), it's a prediction that directly or indirectly causes itself to become true due to positive feedback between belief and behavior. In other words, the self-fulfilling prophecy begins with a *false* definition of a situation that evokes new behavior which makes the original false conception come true. The spurious validity of the self-fulfilling prophecy perpetuates a continuing chain of beliefs and errors, which the so-called prophet can cite as proof that he was right from the very beginning. Sitting at a table, doing his own work at the library, not even interacting with his charges, it has become to Tim's psychological advantage to have these students fail. It's not his fault. It's simply a cause-and-effect scenario. His body posture and his language all convey his central thesis: *These kids are not worth my effort.*

The students are also easy targets. They, too, no longer believe that they are capable learners. Coupled with the self-fulfilling prophecy is the Pygmalion effect. It works like this: Basically, if a person thinks you are clever or stupid or whatever, they will treat you that way. If we are treated as clever, we will act clever; similarly, if we are treated as if we are stupid, we will act, and even become more stupid. When people treat you as if you have certain attributes, you'll behave that way. It doesn't make sense to try to convince people otherwise; it's just easier to live up to those negative thoughts and expectations. The students, then, play their part, showing little interest in achieving anything.

Summer programs in this part of town seem to send a message: Summer is a luxury you can't afford. Despite the best intentions of those who may have created them, these programs in the Badlands seem to accentuate, almost exacerbate, the isolation and limited opportunities for students. If summer programs near Chestnut Hill are characterized by their very sense of "aliveness," here the sense is "deadness." And what's worse, the very people who are supposed to keep their dreams and hopes alive seemed to have given up.

THERE'S SOMETHING INCALCULABLE ABOUT DEVELOPING EXPERTISE. It is inherently motivating. Students don't do it to please others; rather, they do it for themselves. It happens when a topic sparks a special interest. It might be a novel instance, something that they want to know more about, and it leads to digging deeper and beginning to develop a richer knowledge base. It is the same process, even for young children. As intuitive scientific thinkers, you'll find that they seem to have an instinct for seeking out evidence, noticing patterns, drawing conclusions, and building theories. When they have an opportunity, that is.

It's the same small room at Lillian Marrero that we have visited so many times before. But today, something is different. It's quiet. Here sit a group of 5-year-olds, intently listening to a discussion of combustion and gases. They are wearing safety glasses, like those you would see in a science lab. In front of the room is Dan, the "Science in the Summer" man, dressed in shorts, sneakers, and a lab coat. He reminds us strikingly of Bill Nye the Science Guy, only without the bow tie. In bright letters on a nearby whiteboard are the words "physical change, chemical change, atom and element." It seems like pretty heady stuff for 5-year-olds.

Dan's given them a problem to solve. Sitting with a piece of paper in their hands, he asks "Can you make paper stretch?" "Nooo!" The group giggles and squeals with delight. "But what if we changed the physical properties of the paper," and Dan whips out a pair of scissors.

He hands them each a pair of scissors, and asks them to solve the puzzle. It's a pretty complicated task, but the kids handle it well. He talks throughout:

> Dan: Very good! You are amazing! You figured that out all on your own.
> Destiny (referring to her friend Louis): He's slow!
> Dan: It's okay. Everyone goes at their own pace.
> Cinai: I messed up!
> Dan: In science, we don't call it mistakes. In science, it's just "Look! I did something new."

After the kids "stretch" out their papers, Dan says it's time to work on "other kinds of physical changes." He brings out other materials with different physical properties, and then pulls out a cylinder filled with baking soda. He pours the vinegar in the baking soda and the kids do *ohhs* and *ahhs* over the eruption. They talk about the many uses of baking soda in cooking. Dan explains, "What we just saw was a chemical change. How did it happen?" Louis adds, "I think it's because of the pressure. There is nowhere else for it to go."

To our astonishment, now Dan pulls out the periodic table. He gives each kid his or her own smaller version. He talks about the different symbols and colors. "Orange is for gasses, blue is for liquids, white is for . . . ?" "Solids!" the children chime in. He goes on about AU, NAEC, and all the differences among gasses, liquids, and solids, to the children's delight. He then gives them each a penny, a cup of vinegar, and some salt; he asks them what they think will happen. The conversation is lively, not noisy, but energizing as the children try out their ideas in simplified experiments. A solid hour has passed before they take a break.

Watching the entire activity, a colleague of ours later on raises some concerns. "It's great that the kids were so engaged, but his material is way over these children's heads. Come on . . . explaining physical properties . . . to five-year-olds?" How predictable. What immediately comes to mind is this: If this activity had taken place in the Chestnut Hill library, parents and relatives would be chortling over how their little precocious scientists were learning about the periodic table. Here at Lillian Marrero, the worry was that the material was developmentally inappropriate.

Just about the best empirical evidence of whether something is or is not developmentally appropriate, however, is to watch children's behavior. Throughout the entire hour, they were actively engaged, putting together facts that would enable them to develop their scientific reasoning. They were getting a sense of the different kinds of things scientists do in their profession. Dan was helping them to weave together multiple moments of learning into a broader domain. He was supporting their interests and building expertise from everyday activity. To us, he wasn't just any camp counselor. He was a hero.

Clearly, all students begin their years eager to learn, and enthusiastic about new ideas, just like these young children with Dan the science man. Yet we found that these interests and natural proclivities were rarely tapped in the Badlands. Instead, students were treated to a pabulum of mind-numbing activities which appeared to fill up the hours until the summer was over. Numerous studies (Brooks-Gunn, Duncan, & Aber, 1997) have documented the tremendous toll that poverty places on the lives of young children and families. Our observations highlight the toll it may take on those purporting to help them escape its ravages.

IN THIS FINAL PHASE of our work, we found the differences in students' experiences especially stark. In Chestnut Hill, students are provided the resources and opportunities to develop their interests, to deepen their knowledge, and to engage with others in communities of practice. With their abilities to use the Internet fluidly, they are able to build on their knowledge assets in ways that support these activities but do not dominate them. In the Badlands, access to these resources and communities of practice is virtually denied. The social stratification of today's class system has essentially opened up doors for some and closed it for others.

During these long, hot summer months, we did not see the knowledge gap narrow; rather, it appeared to grow ever larger. Not in the conventional sense, however. For example, in an important study, Doris Entwhisle and her colleague Karl Alexander (Entwisle, Alexander, & Olson, 1997) tracked 790 randomly selected 1st-graders in Baltimore, calculating both their achievement score gains in summer, when schools were closed, and their winter gains, when schools were open. Regardless of their socioeconomic status, all students gained substantially during the winter months. However, it was the summer months that were most telling, with affluent students continuing to gain while the less affluent lost ground. The pattern continued throughout the elementary years so that by the time students were about to enter middle school, the differences were stark: the low-SES students gained less than 1 point in reading, whereas the high-SES children had gained 47 points in reading. The authors likened it to a faucet. When school is in season, the faucet is turned on for all children; when school's not in session, poor families cannot make up for the resources the school has been providing, and so their students' achievement either reaches a plateau or falls down.

In our case, the faucet looked more like a deluge. There were vast differences in the experiences for these students who live in geographically concentrated neighborhoods. In the Badlands, for example, programs were so poor that one might question whether they were doing more harm than good. Rather than engage students, these low-quality programs only reify existing stereotypical views of these young teens' capabilities and future opportunities. They focus on deficits and deficiencies, not on students' competencies or curiosities. And while these students are essentially placed on "hold," their peers in Chestnut Hill are being inducted in communities of practice that involve them in the meaningful production of knowledge. Further, these students are learning how to engage in a process of collective learning through technological advances in a shared domain of human endeavor.

Consequently, if it were only a matter of achievement score differences, then remedial exercises might help to close the gap between these two groups. We could simply provide tutorial services to teach students the fundamentals of decoding and comprehension. But what we are seeing is far more deleterious, not measured in achievement scores, but in human capital formation. In this case, some groups of students, in privileged communities, are using the summer months to gain skills far beyond those that are trained in schools; they are learning the benefits of developing expertise, using this know-how to address both the tacit and dynamic aspects of knowledge creation and sharing, as well as its more explicit aspects. Other students, in poor areas, are being left out. These are skills central to the development of information capital that no school will fill and that can never be captured by achievement test scores. These are the mechanisms that are compounding class advantages and disadvantages in this new ecology of inequality.

CHAPTER 8

Conclusions

You can almost anticipate what they will tell you. The stories have a strikingly similar refrain. It starts with grand dreams. It ends with dreams denied. The street-smart clothes, the knock-off designer handbags, and lavish make-up can't disguise what inevitably comes out in their life narratives. Poverty in the Philadelphia Badlands is hardly neutral.

It is here in the library, this glorious institution—where the tethers of social stratification seem to lose their grip—that we hear about these dreams and disappointments. It's not one thing that goes wrong but a confluence of wrong things—poverty, racism, lack of education, barriers to spatial mobility—that appear to shut down their ambitions. But while the causes are many, the effects tend to be the same. Once a people of promise, too many of these young adults are likely to experience a social environment in which poverty and joblessness are the norm and their prospects for social mobility are few. The generalist skills they may have developed within their community will not be prized in an economy that is increasingly dependent on expert thinking and complex communication.

Surely schools have failed them. Take Amy, a Hispanic young woman about 20 years old who we see two or three times a week at the library. She attended high school for a while but left after 9th grade. "I had problems with the teachers. I hated it. I'd say, 'I don't understand. You are going too fast.' But they would just tell me to go away. I tried later to go to get my GED program but I just stopped going to that. I didn't get my diploma." Or Francesca, who dropped out of school in Puerto Rico, only to come here and drop out here: "The school was really bad. They had no books, or papers, nothing and the teachers were bad. All they did was gossip with each other and flirt with the other men teachers." Or Duck, 14, who reportedly likes school, but is thinking of dropping out—"I just don't want to know that stuff they're teaching."

Even some who stick it out, like Crystal who proudly reports that she has "that piece of paper"—the first to graduate high school in her family—doesn't know why she bothered other than to prove to her family that she could do it. Craig, a recent graduate from Martin Luther King high school, only stayed in school to work with his coach who thought he had promise as a welterweight boxer. Emily finished at Edison High School but reportedly hated every last minute of it with the exception of her art classes.

Whether or not they have a high school degree, you might say, is beside the point. They are uneducated. Denied the access to resources, time, and opportunity to learn, these young adults do not have the information capital or its social concomitants that will enable them to successfully engage in well-paid work. Living in a community of concentrated poverty, despair has become the commodity, not hope. Often it appears like there are more drug rehabilitation programs than there are technical training or vocational education opportunities. And as their world becomes increasingly narrow, their goals for gainful employment diminish and the prospect of limited options seems to become a way of life.

Throughout this book, we have seen how these forces of spatial distribution of poverty and privilege influence students' educational opportunities and, ultimately, their aspirations. In this social ecology, affluent people increasingly live, interact, and become educated with other affluent people, while the poor increasingly live, interact, and are educated with other poor people. This new political geography divorces the interests of the rich from the welfare of the poor, creating a more polarized and rigid society. With little day-to-day interactions in community, school, and after-school programs, affluent communities may be unaware of the despair that haunts their neighboring communities like the Badlands, making political solutions and changes all that more untenable.

An incident in one of our last visits to Lillian Marrero underscores these contrasts between communities. We were leaving the library just a few minutes past sunset. Descending the steps to the street level, we turned west to encounter a flashing blue strobe light atop a police surveillance camera, motioning in ways that seemed to follow our every movement. Large, thick drops of dried blood dotted the pavement as we walked to the bus stop. From the curb to the middle of the 10-foot-wide sidewalk, it formed little curlicues, almost as if a gunshot victim had made circles back and around before lurching forward again. The trail turned south, the droplets of blood much closer and bigger than at the start. We reached our destination at the Rite Aid on the corner and waited for our bus.

Moments later, a man in a shirt and tie stepped out of the Rite Aid wheeling a janitor's bucket, brimming with soapy water. "There's blood all the way down the street," a man stationed outside the door of the Rite Aid said to the man in the tie. "It started way back up there," he adds, pointing in the direction from which we had just come. "Yeah, I followed it the last block," someone who was walking ahead of us added, before asking him, "How long it been there?" The man at the door responded, "Maybe last night." Then he points in the direction of where the trail of blood continued and added, "There's a big pool of it down there." As they talked, the man in the tie started scrubbing away right in front of us with the long-handled brush with little success. There were so many drops, thick as paint, saturating the concrete so deeply that even the heavy scraping seemed to do little to erase them. Our bus pulled up and we boarded it.

Most striking to us throughout this incident was how matter-of-factly the men talked and went about their task. If such an event had occurred in the gentrified neighborhood of Chestnut Hill, the mayor, local dignitaries, and police would be swarming to the scene, actively engaged with reporters trailing behind them to gather their every word. People's jobs would be on the line, the local public would be outraged, and everyone would be held accountable until the crime was solved. But here, two lone men were dealing with the latest tragedy in their neighborhood, a story that might not even make the nightly news. Sadly, this event would go down as just one more crime statistic in this outlaw neighborhood known for its frontier-like sense of justice.

These are the draining and disheartening set of circumstances that parents in the Badlands must deal with daily in educating their young children. In such circumstances, when it becomes increasingly difficult to succeed according to conventional standards, students in poor areas may develop what John Ogbu describes as "oppositional identities," to preserve their self-esteem when expectations are low and failure is likely. Success in school may be devalued, hard work considered to be "selling out," and any displays of expertise, unrewarded. Once such an ethos becomes established, it may acquire a life of its own, contributing to the reproduction of poverty, and the cultural transmission of low socioeconomic status.

THE WILLIAM PENN FOUNDATION, to its credit, recognizing the potential of revitalizing neighborhoods like these in Philadelphia–the "city of neighborhoods"–funded a community-based initiative to provide greater access to information and technology. And in many ways, they succeeded masterfully in their efforts. In 5 years, they transformed neighborhood libraries, 32 in all, into technology-rich centers. Today, visiting a neighborhood library, you are likely to find collections that reflect the local culture backed by murals that typify its history, specially designed architectural features that allow for the intimacy of independent reading as well as Internet areas for communities of practice, an abundance of current resources, and throngs of people using its services. Central to their neighborhood, they demonstrate how libraries contribute to the life and vitality of urban communities.

At the same time, despite this enormous effort, the initiative fell short of its goal to close the disparities in resources among communities. Of course, many would reason that the goal was too lofty to begin with, especially given the enormous differences in access to print in our neighborhoods recorded in the outset of our work. However, what became clear throughout our analysis is that while the initiative could greatly improve access to material resources, it could not make up for the intangible psychological resources—the parents and other adults who make the many pathways to reading and information-seeking meaningful and important to children early on.

In their very early years, for example, children were initiated into reading and library activities in different ways. In Chestnut Hill, parents were ever vigilant and seemed to take pride in their scaffolding role, offering help, instruction, and encouragement to their children. Expectations for performance were high but so were the rewards for progress. By contrast, parents in the Badlands appeared to support their children's independent explorations, bringing them to the library to receive instruction from others. These activities appeared to set a pattern of media preferences and habits, with one group of students increasingly using media for information and challenging purposes while the other, reading "down," sought media for entertainment. Soon we began to see a pattern of what we called "the more, the more, the less, the less," an iteration of the Matthew Effect, with students who were able to read fluently reading more and acquiring more information, while other students seemed to develop avoidance strategies, merely tolerating reading without the cognitive involvement associated with reading for comprehension.

Exacerbating these patterns, in the geographic confines of neighborhoods like Chestnut Hill, competition can be fierce. Computers and the Internet seemed to provide the optimal tool to place children on the road to reading earlier on than others. This new type of "play" helped children to develop greater facility with the alphabetic principle, positioning them for reading independently. With technology increasing the flow of information, these students were able to read more and read material of greater difficulty, increasing the speed of gathering information from media sources, while their less-skilled colleagues found themselves embroiled in material that was either too easy or too difficult, delaying the development of automaticity and speed. In the middle grade years, we began to see a sizable knowledge gap, further attenuated by the differences in time and opportunity to use the Internet. By the teen years, these more privileged students were increasingly supported to develop their expertise to become knowledge creators rather than mere knowledge consumers. And by this time, the differences were now immeasurable, with students in one neighborhood effectively mentored into vibrant informational communities which exposed them to many different ideas and interactions, while the other was increasingly consigned to remedial, deadening learning tasks, limiting the potential for the development of information capital.

Consequently, technology appeared to inadvertently reinforce the gap that already existed between students and their families from neighborhoods of poverty and privilege. Further, given the extraordinary capabilities of the new media environment, one could defensibly argue that these conditions actually exacerbated differences in educational opportunity. In short, a new age of inequality is upon us.

CLEARLY, THERE IS NO GOING BACK. The Internet cannot be un-invented; computers cannot be made slower; the demands for expertise will not be reversed. If anything, the pace of technological change will increase dramatically, only reinforcing the needs for new literacies and higher-level reading and thinking skills that have already occurred. Keeping the status quo, however, is also not an option. In doing so, we risk further disenfranchising the poor and alienating them from educational and economic institutions, losing a potentially enormous human resource. To reverse the growing polarization between the so-called haves and have-nots, below we list a number of policy implications, recognizing that they represent only a beginning to a much-needed process of serious thought, reflection, and further debate.

"Un-level" the Playing Field

Too many government program, like Title I, as well as private philanthropy, like the William Penn Foundation, have based their efforts on the flawed policy of "leveling the playing field," giving high-poverty students a leg up by equalizing their educational resources so that they are on par with more affluent communities. Today, the "comparability" provision in federal and state funding programs, for example, is still the tool that officials use to ensure equal educational opportunity among poor and higher-income students. The problem is, however, that the notion of comparability or "leveling" only appears in a situation in which none of the competing partners has an advantage at the outset of a competitive activity. As we have seen, that is certainly not the case for students who come from poor neighborhoods in comparison with their more affluent peers.

Rather, we need to tip the balance on comparability not by equalizing funding but by providing more resources and additional supports to students in poor neighborhoods. As a policy strategy, "resources" are most frequently defined as extra funding. Surely, we have seen that additional funds targeted to more computer and Internet resources in the Badlands would help repair the inequities in access for these students. However, additional targeted human resources are needed as well. Placing more adult mentors in the preschool area in libraries is just one type of additional support that could have enormous implications in the amount, type, and quality of early shared

The Mentoring Adult

reading provided to young children in these low-income communities. Using technology specialists to create knowledge-centered Internet environments, presenting young children early on with challenges just manageable enough to maintain engagement, yet not to lead to discouragement, is another type of additional support. Training assistants to craft opportunities for more intensive engagements with resources is crucial for these children's further learning. Such targeted experiences with human resources, therefore, may include more intensive mentoring, additional adult involvement, more challenging and culturally relevant pedagogy, and learning opportunities associated with quality mother-child interactions, compressing more experiences and practice into the time available.

Parent Involvement Training

Nearly ubiquitous, the story hour in libraries has introduced millions of youngsters to the joys of reading and listening to stories. There is an important role for librarians and teachers to play, as well, in training parents on the skills associated with successful reading. In our experience, parents in the Badlands wanted to provide children with a good start; however, they often didn't know what they could do to help.

building skills in parents

Helping parents understand which skills and capacities children will need to become successful readers builds information capital. It helps in making judgments about what kinds of language and literacy experiences to look for in preschool and child-care settings; what to look for in initial reading instruction in kindergarten and the early grades; what to ask of principals and other policymakers who make decisions regarding reading instruction; and finally, whether their child is making adequate progress in reading or needs additional instruction. The goal is to unlock the mystery of what it takes to ensure children's successful achievement in school.

Once we thought that these early reading skills should be taught in kindergarten, when children were 5 or 6 years old. Now we know that literacy begins in infancy, with a child's first exposure to language, and then progresses in rather predictable ways through language learning, early exposure to books and to the sounds and symbols of language, experimental play with reading, accurate decoding, and fluent reading, all the way to the most advanced forms of reading to learn and constructing meaning from multiple texts. We need to help parents understand the crucial role they play in children's early lives, to think of their role not as a backup teacher or at-home homework "completer," but as a supportive coach and guide in the process of learning to read. The informal literacy lessons they provide for young

Another
Mentoring
Adult

Adult Helping Child to Select a Book

children, by reading to them, telling stories, and cheering on their efforts to learn shape what children know and how they come to see their eventual place of literacy in their own lives. It is imperative that we engage parents in these endeavors.

Computer Training and Assistance

"Googling" may have become common parlance to many people. It is not familiar to all, however, particularly for those in low-income communities. The digital divide is still an unfortunate by-product of living in poor areas where Internet access is often limited or unreliable.

Historically, the role of librarians has been as caretakers of materials, "apostles of culture," and in more recent years, information navigators of the Internet and other digitized collections. Most often, a librarian's educational role has been to serve users by gathering information and providing spaces for learning and reflection. Yet as important as these activities are, Milbrey McLaughlin and her colleagues in their study of public institutions in impoverished communities (McLaughlin, Irby, & Langman, 1994) discovered an additional factor in community-building efforts—caring adults that go beyond their specific job descriptions to take on new roles and responsibilities.

If libraries are to provide equal access to resources for all our citizens, we must consider interventions and training that strategically provide information navigation skills to adults and their young children to promote higher quality uses of the library resources. Recent advances in technology offer extraordinary support for reading development and information-gathering. However, as we have seen throughout our observations, these resources will not be used to full advantage without training and support from adults. There is often the belief that these new technology tools are self-teaching; that pre-readers and beginning readers do not need the careful scaffolding of an adult who may use the clever animations and multimedia characteristics in ways that make the "work" of reading more like play. They are wrong. Even the most comprehensive software cannot substitute for the power of adult guidance and support for enhancing student learning.

Technology supports in federal grant programs have focused on hardware and software, once again making the mistaken assumption that more machines and more technology will improve students' achievement. Rather, training adults to help students make optimal use of these digital resources for information and knowledge creation would be a wiser strategy in the long run.

Access to Information

It seemed like a yearly ritual. Throughout our study, city budget allocations for libraries would be on the cutting block. Particularly in the poorest neighborhoods, budgets would be slashed, and libraries even threatened with closure. Supposedly saving precious taxpayers' dollars, hours of operation would be curtailed, weekends limited, and librarians inevitably asked to do more with less. In essence, access to information for poor families and their children was seen as expendable.

In observing these events, it seems as if we have forgotten how precious libraries are to our society. We expect much of them—from helping us perform our civic duties to understanding our fundamental rights in a democracy—but often we give little in return in terms of public support. Nevertheless, the library as an institution has continued to serve its mission; to support the virtues of information and reading, to offer people opportunities to read what they choose, rather than what is chosen for them. Unlike school, the public library has no predetermined curriculum or pedagogical emphasis; rather, it is designed as neutral space available to all ages and socioeconomic status groups. Historically, this institution has helped to reduce inequity by making information readily accessible to the community at large; today, it is serving this role masterfully as nearly the sole safety net for those who lack access to print and other technologies.

Library closures, limited hours, and diminished services do great harm to all citizens, but especially those in poor neighborhoods. Instead of closing them down, we need to recognize their central role in revitalizing communities, and support them with greater funding. Libraries that serve our most needy communities should be open for more days per week and for more hours per day, with a greater number of resources and services. They serve as a lifeline of information to their local citizens.

Engage Students' Minds

Far too often, people underestimate the capabilities of students who live in poor neighborhoods, equating poverty with low ability. In reality, however, these students are eager to learn and develop greater expertise if given opportunities to do so. It is so rare, unfortunately, that such opportunities are offered to them.

In public policy, our targets for these students have been to help them graduate high school, receive their diploma, and become college-ready. In fact, they will need far more. If these students are to have a fighting chance, they will need a rich knowledge base, a generative mind-set, an ability to deal with a medium that honors multiple forms of intelligence—abstract, textual, visual, musical, social, and kinesthetic. They will need to learn how to participate in a new kind of information fabric in which learning, playing, and creative thinking interact in ways that not only use existing knowledge, but that advances it in new directions. They will need to learn how to work with others collaboratively in teams that better leverage their knowledge assets, taking advantage of the synergy that takes place when diverse people work together. We deceive them and ourselves if we expect any less.

In contrast, what these students are often given is a diet of mindless, remedial-like activities that deaden their intellectual growth and development. Students come to expect less and give less in return. They perceive themselves as poor learners and seek avoidance strategies, whether it is dropping out mentally or physically from school. Rather, these students need adults who believe in their abilities, and trust that they are capable learners. They need programs that help to develop their expertise in domains of interest, immersion in communities of practice, recognizing that enculturation lies at the heart of learning. When we give students opportunities to become involved in cognitively stimulating topics that spark their interests and imaginations, we begin to tap their extraordinary potential.

Economic Integration

Schools today reflect their neighborhoods. In geographically concentrated neighborhoods of poverty, children will attend schools in which over 90% of families are poor. Similarly, in geographically concentrated neighborhoods of affluence, children will attend schools in which over 90% of families are affluent. Throughout our country this pattern persists: schools are economically segregated, further exacerbating the problems of inequality.

If we are truly committed to improving the education of poor children, we will have to get them away from learning environments that are smothered in poverty. Schools in poor areas struggle for many reasons, but among the most prominent is their rotating faculty of inexperienced teachers, low-level curriculum, and ineffectual administrators. In contrast, schools in affluent areas are more stable, with more highly trained teachers, rigorous curriculum, fewer discipline problems, and more support from volunteers.

Studies (Kahlenberg, 2001) have shown that economically integrating schools can be a feasible strategy for changing this scenario. This is being done in some places with impressive results. An important study by the Century Foundation in Montgomery County, Maryland, showed that low-income students who were enrolled in affluent elementary schools performed far better than similarly low-income students in higher-poverty schools in the county. After 7 years, students in low-poverty neighborhood schools cut the large initial gap with middle-class students by half in math and by one-third in reading. Students performed at almost half a standard deviation better than comparable low-income students in higher-poverty neighborhoods and schools. Further, achievement scores for the middle-class students did not decline or show evidence of any negative effects.

It suggests that economic integration of schools could be a powerful lever for raising achievement for poor students, giving them a fighting chance. However, scars from school busing battles have made policymakers and district superintendents leery of raising such issues again. Further, parents with the means to live close to top-performing schools often resist efforts to bring in large numbers of students from poor families. Even so, a growing number of school districts—some say 80 or more—are experimenting with strategies that promote economic diversity that may be more palatable to the middle class. These include specialized technology schools, dual language, and extended day programs that may take into account economic status, giving more students of all backgrounds a way to attend strong, high-quality, and intellectually stimulating schools.

In sum, we have deliberately painted the effects of concentrated affluence and concentrated poverty and its consequences for the development of information capital in bleak terms in this book, not to suggest its inevitability but to galvanize people to action. Without solutions, our economic prosperity is at risk. Without solutions, our image to the world as a just and fair society is even more so.

Breaking Out—
Giving Our Children
a Fighting Chance

In the last half century, our country has become more prosperous (for some), more peaceful (for many), and more fair (for all). At the same time, our social fabric has deteriorated, social trust has plummeted, and our society has become more segmented. According to various pundits, these problems are caused by too much government (the neo-conservatives) or too little (the liberals), too few jobs (economic determinists) or too few values (cultural determinists). Whatever their cause, however, the problems remain the same: Those who are likely to succeed in our society today will have a breadth and depth of information capital; those who do not will be susceptible to the economic waves of disruption that will be more than likely throughout their adult lives.

In recent years, a body of research has emerged that begins to move beyond the identification of problems to offering some solutions. This research supports a few powerful common themes. First, we now have convincing evidence that no matter how poor or impoverished an environment might be, children can learn and thrive when they receive a quality education (Neuman, 2009). Children who grow up in disrupted communities and are at risk can grow up to lead highly productive lives if given opportunities to learn. Second, urban public schools can provide rigorous, academic, content-rich instruction for students all the way from kindergarten through high school (Dobbie & Fryer, 2009). It's simply not true that urban schools should be considered synonymous with dysfunction. Third, teachers matter. Quality teaching has long-term effects on children's lives (Chetty, Friedman, & Rockoff, 2012). Teachers who have shown to be most successful are both caring and demanding. They understand the enormous potential of their students and work to adjust their practices to meet students' needs. The numbers behind these studies might be compelling; even more so when one watches how it all works in action.

IT'S OFTEN CALLED A MIRACLE. You visit an inner-city school and you see amazing results. Students seem intellectually accomplished, achievement scores are up, retention and drop-outs down. Pretty soon pundits hear about it, are dazzled, and try to frame whatever the school is doing into a way that makes it pleasing to the public. Presto _____ (fill in the blank) has become the new educational elixir—the cure-all for all that ails inner-city schools.

The pattern of the magic bullet—whether it's the Texas Miracle, the Harlem Miracle, or some other potion—has plagued the field of educational reform. It's offered single-shot solutions to complicated problems. Develop rigorous common core standards. Extend instructional time. Recruit high-quality teachers. Each of these solutions has potential merit. Standards surely could bring greater coherence and continuity to a program. You'd have to look long and hard to find someone to argue against more time-on-task for learning; and alternative recruiting strategies could breathe some fresh new talent into the teaching force. All good. Nevertheless, for any of these reforms to work, to increase the quality of education, they will need the most central feature of what makes any school really great: a compelling curriculum. Students will ignore noisy hallways, leaky roofs, even the most kind but inexperienced teacher, if they are engaged in meaningful learning.

In the last decade, a school's success has largely been determined by gains in standardized reading and math tests. These scores are now routinely used as if they represent a comprehensive summary of what students know and what the schools produce. However, these kinds of tests were never intended to serve that function; they were originally designed as mere proxies of progress in the foundational skills of reading, writing, and computing. These basic skills might best be described as enablers for the more complex critical analysis and the development of more complex communication. Put these higher-level thinking goals into coursework and involve students in in-depth learning and you won't need miracles. You will have produced sustainable, scalable, and accountable reforms that reflect the true meaning of educational achievement.

HIGH SCHOOLS CAN BE WASTELANDS, confusing labyrinths of activity, open classrooms, hallways going off into nowhere, relentless bells, and interruptions for public announcements—at least to those of us who have spent most of our careers in preschool and elementary school settings. So it took more than a little arm-twisting from Ann Cook, co-director of the Urban Academy Laboratory High School in the Upper East Side area of New York City, to understand why we might want to visit a high school and what we might learn about knowledge-intensive environments, especially as it applies to early education.

Urban Academy is the celebrated Blue Ribbon high school established in 1985 by Deborah Meier in the heyday of Superintendent Tony Alvarado's alternative school reform in New York City. Even today, the school reflects New York's peculiar blend of hard-edged intensity and neighborhood intimacy in its idiosyncratic classrooms, which occupy a second-floor corner of a transformed giant city high school. Immediately you get the sense that this is not your typical high school. Right down to the gauzy Indian prints and tie-dye fixtures along the walls, it has the feel of the 1960s. The long office is crammed with overflowing teachers' desks, and students seated in old couches are locked in conversations throughout the ample hallways. It's known as a transfer school, a secondary placement for the 120 9th- through 12th-grade students who have floundered in other schools.

The design of the school curriculum started with a question: How could school help to develop rather than stunt children's intellectual curiosity? Meier's belief was that poor children, in particular, were being driven into dumbness by a failure to challenge their curiosity, to build on their natural drive toward competence (Meier, 2002). Her answer was to build a curriculum that demanded intellectual toughness—not just for the children, but for the teachers as well. Classes needed to support in-depth teaching, longer periods, and exhibitions that could thoughtfully and demonstrably highlight students' proficiencies in logical thinking, argument, and writing. In fact, whereas typically the higher the student body's economic status the meatier the curriculum, the more open-ended the discussion, the less rote and rigid the pedagogy, the more respectful in tone, and the more rigorous the expectation, Meier wanted to change the equation providing these experiences to low-income students.

The pedagogy in this school is inquiry-based, centered on asking hard questions and looking for answers—but that would be selling the program short. It is about the power of ideas and the habits of mind that shape the curriculum. Classes remind us of seminars, with students and the teacher sitting in a circle having intellectual conversations. Visiting a class on the American Indians, we listen to the conversation of the students who are reviewing their notes on a film they just went to see. The teacher poses a question, "Who is a real Mohawk Indian?" Jeemia reflects on the underlying problem, saying, "I understand that the Mohawks want to continue their race, and it's a problem that race is getting watered down. They're under a lot of pressure to keep things well-defined." "Yes, but this can lead to more racism," says Maleque. "I feel like there's a lot of racism around—like you kind of have to fit into someone else's criteria." But then Jeremiah adds, "There's a rule in this country if you are less than half Indian then you can't be Indian. But someone like that might know more about being an Indian than someone who is part of the total culture. I think that cultural practices should be the determining factor. If you adhere to the rituals you should be allowed to be an Indian." We follow the conversation as it continues about culture and its ramifications, reasoning that we must be witnessing an Advanced Placement course for gifted students–that is, until we hear that there are no such distinctions among courses or students.

Getting kids to question is an important feature of an inquiry approach. But a good question must be based on knowledge. Students are given reading assignments not from textbooks but from primary resources, and asked to weigh these sources of information. Discussions are often about evaluating facts and developing opinions on topics that are timely and relevant. We visit a class called "Show Me the Money," which turns out to be a foundational economics course. Today, Avram and Adam, two of the teachers, are holding a debate about President Obama's economic plan. The question on the floor is, "Will President Obama's Treasury Secretary Geitner's plan to rescue the nation's banks actually work?" Students are seated in a circle around the teachers. Adam, one of the teachers, goes to the board and talks about capital and liabilities and that the bank now has a series of toxic assets. "And so the question is, how to help the banks so that they do not become insolvent and to get the private equity firms and the hedge funds to begin to invest again."

The teachers present their arguments, one for the plan, the other against, while the students take notes throughout the debate. Then they turn it over to the students, who begin to question their arguments. One student comments, "Why should we fund failure? Once they bail out all the assets, what's to stop the banks from giving bad loans again?" Another, "Why should the hedge funds be the only ones to invest–why couldn't they create gigantic pools of groups and allow normal citizens to invest in a portion of the recovery?" Avram replies, "That's an interesting idea; I have to study this more." Another, "What we really need to happen is getting some cash flow in the country. While Obama's plan isn't perfect it seems it's the best plan we have." Still another asks, "Well why isn't it good to nationalize the banks, I don't see it as the problem?" To which another replies, "There's a country called Russia" (everybody laughs) and adds, "But if the banks themselves buy the assets, what happens to fundamental capitalism?"

It's the quality of the language, reasoning, and students' grappling with fundamental concepts that is so striking and refreshing in each of the classes we visit. There's an energy that comes from the students, and the teachers who learn from them, that you too rarely see in many school settings. Knowledge is dynamic, used to generate novel ideas. Following the debate, every week students write in-class essays that connect to the issues being debated, encouraging students to engage in the kind of time-limited, pressured writing experiences that they can expect to encounter in college.

But it's not just the students who seem so engaged; it's the teachers as well. It could well be the opportunity that the Academy offers these teachers to turn their interests, knowledge, and passions into curriculum coursework. You won't find your average Literature 101, or Fundamentals of Biology courses here. You won't find a script. Rather, in their ever-changing course catalog, you'll see "Shakespeare Goes to the Movies," a course where students and the teacher compare Shakespeare's plays with their movie counterparts and examine choices that screen writers and directors make when they adapt Shakespeare to film. Or instead of your basic science, you'll find a course called "Human Diseases," a class that tries to figure how disease invades the human immune system, and asks whether they are caused by internal or external factors, such as invading organisms, bacteria, parasites, and fungi. It's the pursuit of knowledge that is the driving force here, not some letter grade or achievement score.

The school has received all sorts of accolades for its innovative use of performance assessments, small class sizes, its involvement in New York City's cultural opportunities, and more. All important. Still, what turns our scheduled 1-hour visit into a day-long visit here is that we watch how students react when they are challenged by ideas, when their viewpoints are considered with respect by other students and teachers, and when curriculum is seen as dynamic and not deadly: students' eagerness to take on rigorous intellectual work.

As we are about to leave, we happen to meet a 4th-grade teacher at the Center for Inquiry, another school in the Education Complex. The teacher starts to describe how she established a debate class along the lines of Urban Academy's "Looking for an Argument" class for her students. The topic is about whether or not a zoo is a humane environment for animals. Soon after, her conversation is interrupted, taken over by one of her students who wants to give us a more detailed blow-by-blow description of his preparation for the debate, the analyses he conducted, as well as the report he wrote up for the school's newsletter. As he describes his research with such animation and enthusiasm, the teacher beams with pleasure. She doesn't need an achievement test to tell her whether or not this student has learned. Rather, we see what an achievement test can never capture: the power and joy of having wonderful ideas.

JOURNALISTS AREN'T THE ONLY ONES who look for miracles. Educators are culpable as well. Far too often, we take a set of ideas on educational reform and reduce them into single magic bullets: whole language, authentic learning; small schools, and more. Pretty soon, we're on a wild trajectory of reforms, costing millions of dollars and upending any stability in our schools.

Remarkably, we see this in outsider's descriptions of places like the Urban Academy. It becomes known as the hallmark of the small school, and Deborah Meier becomes known as the small-school pioneer. However, the multiple dimensions of reform that are more foundational to its success are glossed over. It may be that the structural move of creating the small school adds to the quality of the interactions among students and students with teachers—but at its best, the fact that it is a small school is not a sufficient condition for educational reform. It's what goes into the small school that matters. Urban Academy's excellence derives from a robust curriculum, a faculty that places high demands on student performance, and a set of beliefs about students' abilities. It recruits teachers who recognize that good teaching is about introducing students to the world of knowledge through active engagement; teachers who show not only a strong knowledge of their subject matter but of human development and the wisdom of the classroom. You don't need a miracle cure to figure out why Urban Academy's students do well, with 94% going on to attend 4-year colleges. You can see it on the sandwich boards that say "I am proficient," as each student parades throughout the hallway with bells loudly ringing, this time celebrating the joy of accomplishment.

ALONG WITH TALK OF MIRACLES, we have those who believe in only one educational wonder drug at a time. Charter schools are the current magical charms, but there have been others before. The problem is that one size doesn't fit all, not for children and their parents, nor for teachers. Place an Urban Academy teacher in the newest elixir of "paternalism" schools, and they would probably not last a day. Place an "Excellence" teacher from one of the growing conglomerates of KIPP-like academies in Urban Academy, and they wouldn't know what to make of the curriculum or its measurement of student work.

All cut from the same cloth, KIPP, Excellence, and Achievement First couldn't serve as a more stark contrast to Urban Academy. Replace the tie-dyes with real ties and white shirts neatly tucked in at the waist. Replace performance goals with test-prep and test-taking. Replace seminars with students seated in rows raising their hands. Replace the small town 1960-ish feel with that of the military. Together, it means that you are entering a new breed of school: one that proudly hearkens to a paternalistic ethos. By paternalistic, we mean a highly prescriptive institution that teaches students not just how to think but how to act according to middle-class values (Whitman, 2009). Rather than fight the inequities in society, they acknowledge them and train their students to achieve excellence through diligence, concentration, and a strong work ethic. And for some, these paternalistic schools seem to represent the single best solution for closing the achievement gap.

It might be described as positivism to the nth degree: These schools teach students how to live. Much in the manner of a benevolent parent, they tell students that they need "attitude adjustment." Throughout the buildings, you'll see messaging aimed at serving their agenda: Work hard, be nice, be honest, believe, develop self-control, all designed to be inspirational while bordering on the propagandistic. For those who don't conform to its messages, detention, two times a day, is never far away.

These schools have clearly adapted the "broken windows" theory of crime reduction to school. James Wilson and his colleague George Kelling (Wilson & Kelling, 1982) discovered that signs of public disorder—graffiti, gangs hanging out on street corners, homeless people loitering in alleys—seemed to create a public perception of disorder. Once these things are cleaned up, people feel safer. The same thing seems true here in these schools. On our visit to the Excellence School in Bedford-Stuyvesant, our host picks up a paper that might have been slightly larger than a keypunch hole, carefully wads it, and places it in a wastebasket. Hallways are spotless, bathrooms immaculate, and the noise level most approximating the low voices of a library.

Inside the classrooms at Excellence, students are practicing their test-taking skills. An assessment team has carefully reviewed the Regents Tests students will have to take to graduate high school, questions from the National Assessment of Educational Progress (NAEP), and others along the way, to develop a list of vocabulary, specific skills, and test-taking strategies to prepare them throughout their schooling. On this particular day, kindergartners are practicing their "bubbling"—how to fill out their answers, what to do if there is an erasure, and what to do if they need to change their minds. In each of the classrooms we visit, teachers are diligently preparing students for yet another test strategy.

The teaching philosophy is straight from tough love. Teachers are stern, well-dressed, and formal. Absolutely no infractions are tolerated, so much so that you'll often hear disciplinary comments throughout the teachers' lessons, such as: "If you can't sit in a chair the right way, I don't have a chair for you." Lessons are directed to the whole group in lectures peppered with questions throughout. Students raise their hands, and as one student responds, all others are supposed to listen, designated by their eyes on the responder. If a student does not follow along, the teacher stops and immediately addresses the issue: "What's so important about the floor, so that you are stopping the whole class from learning?" The student either focuses or is asked to leave the room. Following the lesson, the assignment is given: "There's to be no speaking. I am coming around with today's class work. You are to sit and read silently. When you silent read, you are to sit up with your back to the chair."

You wouldn't say that the curriculum or instruction is particularly inspiring. At KIPP Academy in the Bronx, the science class begins with a carefully prepared set of objectives. "Today we will identify parts of an ecosystem. We will analyze changing populations." Students are given a worksheet and asked to put their homework out on their desk. The teacher walks around the room, checking to see if homework is complete, reminding students that "I want it quiet" and "There is to be no talking." She returns the previous day's test, and asks those who received a 90 to 100 to stand up. As she says their names, the children give two claps, a sign of excellence, while those below 90 look on. Twenty-five minutes have passed before the lecture begins.

Moving on to the literature class, you'll find a similar format. Today, the students are learning about Shakespeare. Standing by the overhead projector, a student is underlining the sentences as the teacher reads aloud. The other 34 students follow along, while the teacher explains each line. At various points, the teacher looks at a student and says, "Should I stop? You need to show respect. I don't see respect. Feet on the floor, back on the seat; eyes on the speaker." Perpetrators are sent out the door for a 5- to 7-minute detention break. After a few more infractions, the teacher closes her book and says to the class, "I'm trying everything to work with you and your energy. We need more self-control from individuals." She ends the lesson by assigning the homework for the next day. One student quietly moans. Pivoting toward him, she responds, "I don't expect a sixth grader to respond like that. I expect self-control." No touchy-feely idealism about critical thinking here. It's all about the enforcement of order.

In fact, the most distinctive feature of these schools is their clarity of teachers' expectations. No guesswork, there's a formula: High achievement + exceptional behavior = Success. To meet these expectations, lessons are extraordinarily prescriptive; curbing student behavior, a primary goal. Even in the middle school, we see 8th-graders lined up, walking from class to class silently, with books by their side. If they talk, they are admonished. "When you are doing what I am asking," or "when you are ready to enter the classroom, we can begin our instruction." We watch as students practice lining up again and again, with the teacher saying, "It is not my problem that you are wasting sixteen minutes of class time; it is your problem. It is your choice." After what seems like an hour, the teacher formally welcomes each student, "Good afternoon, Tanya," shaking his or her hand as each enters the classroom, now apparently ready for learning.

The curriculum is dry and demanding. Adhering strictly to state standards and outcomes, you might say it goes farther than parochial schools in its focus on the nuts and bolts of learning—grammar, classics, computation. But interestingly, the schools make no apologies for it. You'll not find teachers engaged in motivational activities or trying to enliven the content in ways to make it more relevant or more exciting. Rather, what you'll see in the design of the curriculum is a focus on a central message: Students, this is what you are going to need in order to be successful.

You'll find a palpable sense of accomplishment among the students. Weekly community meetings celebrate individual and group triumphs. At Excellence, they use what they call a "spirit stick," some old dilapidated bed post from a local yard sale that they've decorated with great resourcefulness to highlight a student's accomplishments each week. It's given to the student not only for gains in achievement but for the values he or she has embraced throughout the week, such as promoting team spirit or helping others. In a ceremony, the award is accompanied by a video montage of interviews from teachers to celebrate the student's activities.

It would be disingenuous for us to say that we enjoyed these visits. Lessons were long and repetitive. Discipline bordered on the harsh and was ever-present. The old teachers' tale of never smiling until Thanksgiving seemed still in effect in March. It wasn't much fun.

Nevertheless, what is pertinent about KIPP academy and throughout similar paternalistic schools is a highly impressive set of findings. There are tangible results. For example, an independent evaluation of 22 KIPP schools in 2010 found that the impacts on students' state assessment scores in mathematics and reading were positive, statistically significant, and educationally substantial. Half of these KIPP schools are producing impacts large enough to cut the Black-White test score gap in mathematics in half within 3 years. Three-year impacts in reading are also large in many KIPP schools, though not as large as the effects in math.

There have been claims by some that these institutions "cherry-pick" their students; that is, they select the best of the bunch from schools that serve low-income children. Others suggest that their placement in school lotteries is indicative of a more active and involved parent than one would typically see in poor schools. Still others claim that they teach to the test and that gains on yearly achievement scores aren't really all that revealing. We find none of these arguments particularly compelling.

Instead, we think another mechanism is at work. In their diligence to maintain order and curb all distractions from learning, these schools seem to be setting the stage for students to begin to regulate their own behaviors. In fact, we would argue that regulation is what they teach–an a priori set of skills that enable knowledge to be acquired.

Studies now show that self-regulation is a deep, internal mechanism that enables students to engage in mindful, intentional, and thoughtful behaviors. There are two sides to it: first, it involves the ability to control one's impulses and to stop doing something. For example, learning not to blurt out an answer when the teacher asks a question takes some self-control. Second, self-regulation involves the capacity to do something (even if one doesn't want to do it) because it is needed. We listened to eight students practicing their scales in front of a class of 35. All 27 students were required to hold their instruments but not play them for 50 minutes. Self-regulated students can delay gratification, and suppress their immediate impulses enough to think ahead of the possible consequences of their action or to consider alternative actions that would be more appropriate. Students learn not only that it's important to listen to others in class discussion; they learn to track the conversations with their eyes and to nod their heads to show that they are listening. This ability to inhibit one's behavior while engaging in a particular behavior on demand is a skill used not just in social interactions but in thinking (cognitive self-regulation as well). Both have neural roots and with exercise, both increasingly develop as students take control of their thinking and their feelings.

Paternalistic schools like KIPP academies and other charter networks like them have recognized that self-regulation is a critical underlying skill that makes learning possible. Without self-regulatory skills, you cannot address the gaps in knowledge. These schools create a safe, secure, respectful environment in which students can learn. They offer a demanding core curriculum that is aligned to rigorous standards, specifying very clearly the performance goals that are expected. Not unlike Urban Academy, they hire teachers who do everything in their power to enable students to be successful, monitoring and supporting them along the way. And while their approach seems more than 180 degrees apart from what you're likely to see at Urban Academy, the results are the same: Students who have the knowledge and skills to go on to be successful.

THERE MAY NOT BE A MAGIC BULLET. But there is one thing that schools of excellence for low-income students share: a deeply rooted belief that academic achievement must be based on content knowledge. No matter how hard teachers may work on teaching higher-level reasoning or critical thinking skills, nothing will "stick" if students don't have the requisite background knowledge to build to a larger storehouse of information.

P.S. 254 in Queens, New York, a school with over 650 students, 70% of whom are on free lunch, started out with the district's "balanced literacy" reading instruction program, meaning that it incorporated both a wide array of literature and phonics instruction into lessons that teach students how to read. But they were finding it wasn't sufficient. Even though good teachers were teaching a good program, students still weren't doing particularly well in comprehension and the more complex skills of synthesizing ideas and making interpretations. The school was more or less at a standstill—good but not great in closing the gap with other schools.

So the staff, along with the help of Kathleen Cashin, a veteran superintendent, voted to adopt E. D. Hirsch's Core Knowledge program (Hirsch, 1996). The program is heavily focused on content, vocabulary skills, and nonfiction books, and is based on the belief that when students struggle in reading, it's largely due to a lack of basic knowledge in subjects like history, science, and literature.

Here's what you're likely to see in a Core Knowledge school: an emphasis on content and the coordination of curriculum throughout all the classrooms in the school. Students of all ages, from kindergarten through middle school, get a heavy dose of history, geography, science, music, visual arts, and mathematics.

It's the transparency of the curriculum that first gets your attention. You'll see standards prominently placed in the classroom that highlight the current content focus. Records of practice are everywhere in what they call "anchor charts." Teachers record their activities and the processes they have used to reach the particular standard. Entering one classroom, for example, the teacher begins, "Let's see what our goal will be on this lesson in math." Near her, on the bulletin board, she reviews the processes they have worked on thus far to meet their goal. The charts reveal: First the students were asked to visit a pretend store and determine what they wanted to buy. Next, they were asked to show the coins that they would use to buy it. Then they were asked to graph the most popular item. "Today, we are working toward interpreting the graph by using the words *compare* and *contrast*." Importantly, other kindergarten classrooms in the same school are working on the same exact objective.

Core Knowledge doesn't focus on how to teach. That's left to the teachers. Rather, it focuses on what to teach and provides a detailed sequence on when to do so. Visiting a 3rd-grade classroom, we find the teacher working on a pretty complex literary topic—*onomatopoeia,* a word that mimics the sound of its own meaning, like *meow* or *buzz.* Here, 25 students—all low-income—are writing poems sprinkled with onomatopoeias after having studied "The Bells" by Edgar Allen Poe. It's made easy because the children have been given the background knowledge needed to be successful.

Because of the carefully developed sequence of content standards, instruction builds on what has been learned from the previous grade year. It's not the same old "let's cut feathers to make an Indian headdress" year in and year out that you often see in school curriculum. We visit a 4th-grade class visual arts class where they are studying about the Renaissance. You see artwork everywhere, and the students are working in "think, pair, share" to examine how math is integrated in the art. Worried that this kind of integration might confuse children, we ask one of the students to tell us about the "Mona Lisa." She describes a bit about the artwork, and its artist, and we then ask, "Where might we find it?" "I think it's in the Sistine Chapel," she begins, then quickly corrects herself. "Actually, it's in the Louvre [said correctly] in Paris," her confidence speaking volumes.

Classroom discussions are filled with what teachers call "purposeful talk"–talk that extends the goals of the lesson. One student holds up her hand and says "I would like to elaborate," and comments about the lesson. She then selects another student who might want to extend or challenge the comment: "I agree with that comment and would like to extend . . . " It reminds us of the self-regulatory focus of the paternalistic schools with a somewhat different twist. Here, teachers work on the "gradual release of responsibility," encouraging students to look deeply at the topic, explore it thoroughly, and make the text to real-world connections on their own.

Much like the other Core Knowledge schools we visited, there is something inherently galvanizing for students when they are mastering a rich and demanding curriculum. Remarkable things begin to happen. In P.S. 108, the 6th-grade students gave us an impromptu performance from *As You Like It,* acted out with great ease and composure to the delight of its unexpected audience. In P.S. 124, located in a high-poverty, high-crime neighborhood that is entered rarely and cautiously by outsiders, the students treated us to a rendition of "mad hot ballroom" dancing in which they're planning to compete. You watch as they concentrate on their moves, clearly enjoying the attention and the effort and time it takes to excel in their performance.

Although these students might arrive with disadvantages, they leave with some of the highest achievement scores in the city. And their culture of success seems pervasive. Not only are these schools educating their students who have been characterized as hard to teach. They are also keeping alive the ideal that content-rich schools with their rigorous standards and demanding curriculum can be engines of opportunity for all students no matter their economic status.

In August 26, 2008, the *New York Times* ran the headline "10 City Schools to Focus Reading Skills on Content." Recognizing the "knowledge deficit," particularly among middle-school students, it was announced that Chancellor Joel Klein had decided to shift from a curriculum of balanced literacy to a pilot a program that focused on content, vocabulary, and world knowledge. The article also suggested that this same problem might be common throughout other middle schools around the country.

Take a moment to consider this headline. Now ask: Why has it take so long to recognize that content must be the centerpiece of curriculum? Moreover, isn't this the central mission of the school, at all levels–to provide rich and meaningful learning experiences? Why has this mission become derailed too often, leading to vague or bland standards, incoherent curriculum that varies from classroom to classroom, or no useful curriculum at all? And finally, why is this a major headline?

The answer is that for decades, perhaps even a century, educators have argued about how to teach rather than what to teach. We have focused on teaching styles, not content. Two stylistic perspectives have dominated the discourse on teaching. On the one side of the continuum is constructivism, the notion that understanding or comprehension of ideas only comes when students learn for themselves from hands-on experiences without direct instruction. From the examples above, you'd more or less typify the Urban Academy, which prides itself on inquiry learning as based on constructivist principles. On the other hand, there is the philosophy of direct instruction. Here, the teacher guides students through instruction, often breaking down a complex problem into more understandable elements or chunks. Paternalistic schools like KIPP, Excellence, and to a large extent Core Knowledge follow a more direct instructional approach. Put simply, there is a body of knowledge to be learned, and students need to acquire it.

What is especially ironic about this either-or philosophy is that none other than John Dewey (1948), often considered the father of constructivism, recognized the destructive nature of such simplistic thinking. Dewey started out as a constructivist, placing the child rather than the teacher as the core of the learning experience. But he began to modify that view as soon as he opened his experimental school in Chicago. He concluded, finally, that education rested on two interacting factors: the immature mind of the child and the organized knowledge of the adult. Simply put, he recognized that you need both, a single process that incorporates the curiosity and inventiveness of the child and the formal knowledge of the teacher.

It is this focus on style rather than content that has often derailed progress in school reform. If this were only a heated debate behind the ivy walls of the university then we could all engage in "reading wars" as if it were the latest sport. But it's not. The lack of quality curriculum has been damaging across the board—for elite students who go on to college as well as for those who choose a vocational field. It hurts in very practical ways. A successful housepainter must be able to do basic geometry to bid on a job. A technician must know how to make basic mathematical computations. A lawyer must be able to make a logical argument in oral and written form. A voter must be able to read a ballot and critically understand the issues. Civil society is based on having the knowledge and understanding of our foundational principles and democratic values in order to make wise decisions.

It is true. Given a choice of where *we* would teach, it would be the Urban Academy, hands down. It fits with our personal views of learning. We enjoyed its hard-edged intellectual push for both students and teachers. It reminded one of us of our training at the University of California, Berkeley. It felt right.

But the point is that it's not about us. It's about educating a great diversity of students. The rhetoric about quality education simply cannot rest on a single model. Paternalistic schools may not be to our personal taste, but they serve students well. The percentages of students who stay through high school and go on to college is laudable. No one would claim that students are forced to attend such schools. Rather, the schools are options that thousands of children and their families have chosen to attend. Based on the waiting lists alone, this option is important to these families who care deeply about their children's future.

Similarly, the Core Knowledge schools, often rejected by constructivists who disparage any notion that there might be a canon of knowledge that all students should know, offer a powerful option. Teachers know what they're supposed to teach. Students know what they are supposed to learn. The steps in the process toward the goals are carefully laid out. The curriculum is sequenced. Students are given background knowledge on who a major figure is, like Martin Luther King and his major accomplishments, for example, before reading his stirring letter from the Birmingham jail. You might expect that this is a common feature in all our schools, but it's often not.

In fact, a sequenced, specific curriculum throws light on a complaint often heard today about accountability, specifically the problem of standardized tests. You'll hear that teachers teach to the test. But in many cases, the reason is as follows. It is not necessarily the existence of tests. Rather, it's the lamentable absence of curriculum. If there's no coherent curriculum, one that details not only horizontal alignment of skills in one grade but vertical alignment from grade to grade, then a test offers the only clear road map of what to teach.

Each of the schools detailed in this chapter approaches the challenges of educating schools differently. But each provides students with a coherent curriculum that not only permits but requires both breadth and depth. It is not about constructivism or direct instruction. This debate has been highly injurious to social justice and the common good. Rather, it is about making transparent in some form or another the foundational knowledge and skills that will allow students to become successful in learning. It's not a miracle. It's about giving all students the fighting chance they all so richly deserve.

Appendix

In 1998, the William Penn Foundation commissioned us to examine the long-term impact of major transformations in library services and technology for enhancing students' access to information through print, multi-media, and electronic resources. Specifically, the foundation was interested in addressing the following key issues:

- How might the physical design changes in local library branches influence social interactions among students?
- How might the greater comprehensibility of services offered to families and communities influence their participation in library services?
- Might greater access to information and technology close the gap for children living in disadvantaged neighborhoods compared to those in the more advantaged circumstances?
- What might be the impact/effects of these library enhancements on library interactions and library uses?
- How does the Philadelphia modern urban library system compare with other programs in other major cities?

Assessing the project's outcomes in achieving these goals represented a culmination of many different data sources, from statistics on specific library uses and naturalistic studies to conducting large-scale surveys of library activities across the country. Our focus was to determine whether libraries were serving an increased educational function for a new audience—an audience that may not have traditionally frequented the local library before. These data were particularly critical when we considered the library's potential to improve students' achievement in the more disadvantaged neighborhoods of Philadelphia, where schools had chronically failed to improve achievement.

It was at this time that we began our ethnographies of selected libraries. Our naturalistic observations offering rich and detailed descriptions of activities within libraries proved to be invaluable in helping us to understand the range and variety of library use. We visited a wide variety of sites regularly, informally, interviewing librarians, children, and staff to develop profiles of library use and users. We conducted in-depth analyses of each section of the library to examine both the uses of reading and its potential displacement with the increasing uses of technology.

Whereas naturalistic studies can provide detailed descriptions of library activities, surveys may estimate how typical or atypical particular uses may be. We conducted a large-scale survey to examine how the enhanced library system compared with similar programs using computer technology in other major cities. Key questions raised in this analysis included: Does Philadelphia's urban library system represent the state-of-the-art in library services? Might the technological system and support provided to children and families be regarded by experts as leading edge? Information was examined first from the initial site visit reports. Additional information was gathered from selected project leaders in key cities. In-depth interviews were conducted to determine the technical quality, level of support provided to the public, and uses of technology and its relation to community needs and organizations. Therefore, through a mosaic of methodologies, the study was designed to provide a rich and comprehensive analysis of the impact of an enhanced library system for the William Penn Foundation and the processes and potential outcomes for improving the equity and educational opportunity of children and families in Philadelphia.

Below, we briefly detail each of these studies, and urge those who are interested in greater detail on the particular methodologies to refer to the articles in our references.

Studies Conducted Throughout the 12-Year Period (1998–2010)

1. *Ethnographies*: We selected eight key libraries throughout our work, four in disadvantaged communities and four in advantaged communities. For 20 hours per week, members of our research team would record all activities in the library over 5 years. This analysis provided a detailed account of how libraries work in these communities.

2. *Frozen time checks*: To understand the changes brought about by technology, we began a series of frozen time checks in these key libraries before technology came; right after it took place; and then finally, after the novelty had worn off. To conduct our frozen time checks on the hour, we would count the number of patrons in the building and observe what they were doing. This gave us a detailed account of activity in the library over a typical week. We conducted these frozen time checks at strategic times throughout our study to better understand how technology influenced patron behavior.

3. *Shadowings*: To understand the various roles of library personnel and the activities they engage in during an average week, we shadowed

the head librarian in each library, the children's librarian, the security officers, and other aides, each for a week. This allowed us to understand the responsibilities of each position as well as how these people often interacted with the local patrons.

4. *Exemplary librarians:* From our shadowings, we then selected children's librarians who seemed to go beyond their particular job description in the ways in which they connected with children. Many of them, for example, set up chess clubs, writing clubs, and community service activities, which seemed to draw nontraditional library patrons to their libraries.

5. *Annual reports:* Each library was responsible for writing an annual report of their activities and involvement in the community. These documents became an excellent dataset to examine differences in turnstile counts and library use across the 32 local library branches we examined.

6. *Community profiles:* Library branches were responsible for developing a demographic description of their community. These community profiles provided us with information on the catchment area, the local culture, and resources in the immediate neighborhood.

7. *Signage:* We walked every block in eight catchment neighborhoods, looking particularly for logographic signs (pictures and words, e.g., McDonald's). We recorded the number and condition of each sign in the neighborhood in order to examine children's exposure to environmental print.

8. *Book audit:* Related to developing a better understanding of the amount of print exposure existing in each neighborhood, we visited every store in these catchment areas in which one could conceivably buy a children's book—whether it be a comic book, a coloring book, or a storybook. We then counted the number of different titles to get some measure of the degree of choice in book selections in different neighborhoods across the city.

9. *Public places (spaces) for reading:* We randomly selected a number of laundromats, bus stops, train stations, diners, etc., to visit to get a sense of whether reading was an activity that would be supported in that environment. For example, in a diner we found newspapers easily available for re-reading; and in hair and nail salons, magazines for browsing. We were interested in understanding whether a child might observe someone reading in a public space across different neighborhoods.

10. *School libraries:* We visited schools in each of the eight catchment areas to examine the condition of the school library. We examined the number of books in these libraries (when there were libraries, that is), their condition, and whether or not they employed a trained librarian.

11. *Preschools and child-care centers*: Similarly, we observed using the *Early Childhood Environmental Rating Scale* the quality of materials and books in local child-care centers in the eight catchment areas. Our analysis of school libraries and preschool environments was designed to help us understand the quantity and quality of print exposure in disadvantaged and more advantaged communities.

12. *In-library use studies*: For each activity pocket (e.g., adult area; preschool area), we developed a methodology that would help us compare and contrast activities across different libraries. Often we used 40 hours (i.e., an average week) as a designated time period in each particular area. We would measure activity, such as adult reading, by recording each and every reading material selected, the number of minutes spent per activity, and the content (e.g., fiction, nonfiction) of the selection. This would allow us to examine whether nonfiction might be privileged in certain communities as compared to fiction, for example. It also allowed us to examine whether or not a parent would be present in a particular activity pocket such as the preschool areas.

13. *After-school sessions*: Since libraries are deluged with patrons right after school lets out, we conducted a naturalistic study of the LEAP program, one specifically focused on how students do homework in the library environment. To do so, we shadowed the LEAP leaders in two of our libraries, and compared our observations across settings.

14. *Camera project*: To examine students' perceptions of their favorite activities, we gave 20 students in each of our focal libraries a camera and asked them to take a week's worth of pictures of their favorite activities. We then interviewed all the students and asked them to describe their leisure preferences and compared these across contexts.

15. *Man on the street interviews*: We were interested in understanding reasons for using or not using the library. We stood in a popular intersection and interviewed adults on why or why not they used the library in their community.

16. *Patron use study*: Standing immediately outside libraries in four different areas, we counted the number of books parents or caregivers checked out. We were particularly interested in their rationale for check-out (or not). Previously we had suspected that check-out was related to the demographic characteristics of the local neighborhood. In these communities, we learned that checking out books was highly related to parents' concerns about late fees. In poor communities, parents were far less likely to check books or videos out because of these concerns.

17. *Summer reading program*: In this study we compared how poor students fared in the summer reading program. We also examined the number of books they were likely to read if they participated in the library

program compared with other options in the local community such as the Salvation Army camp.

18. *Summer camp*: We visited camps in the local area in Chestnut Hill and the Badlands. Given concerns about "summer reading loss," we observed and recorded activities for students and their different options throughout the summer.

19. *Computer use studies*: Using momentary time sampling, we examined teenagers' use of computers–the amount of print they read–the selections of activities in 13 different libraries. Our interest was to determine whether there were differences among student choices and reading selections in disadvantaged compared to advantaged communities.

20. *Computer access in neighborhoods*: Given the extraordinary demand for computer time at the Lillian Marrero library, we conducted an audit of community-based organizations to determine if there were other venues for providing students access to computers. We visited all local organizations and calculated the amount of time and the quality of computer access for students and children in the area.

21. *Survey of library services and resources*: We compared library services and resources in ten major cities through an online survey and we visited several exemplar programs. Our goal was to better understand how the library system and its transition to technology in Philadelphia compared with other major cities.

In total, these 21 studies provided an enormous wealth of data, both qualitative and quantitative, to determine how libraries enter into people's lives. We hope that we have done it justice.

Finally, we could not have chosen a more inspirational and motivational place to do our work. We sincerely wish to acknowledge all the unnamed individuals in these library branches who have helped us over these many years and who continue to work unceasingly for children and their families. They are the hidden stars of Philadelphia.

References

Adams, M. (2010). Advancing our students' language and literacy. *American Educator, 34*(4), 3–10, 53.

Anderson, D., & Collins, P. (1988). *The impact on children's education: Television's influence on cognitive development* (Working Paper No. 2). Washington, DC: Office of Educational Research and Improvement.

Anderson, E. (1999). *Code of the street.* New York: W.W. Norton.

Arafeh, S., Levin, D., Rainie, L., & Lenhart, A. (2010). *The digital disconnect: The widening gap between Internet-savvy students and their schools.* Washington, DC: Pew Internet and American Life Project.

Ball, S., & Bogatz, G. (1970). *The first year of Sesame Street: An evaluation.* Princeton, NJ: Educational Testing Service.

Beentjes, J. (1989). Learning from television and books: A Dutch replication study based on Salomon's model. *Educational Communication and Technology Journal, 37*(1), 47–58.

Beentjes, J., & Van der Voort, T. (1988). Television's impact on children's reading skills: A review of research. *Reading Research Quarterly, 23*(4), 389–413.

Bereiter, C. (2002). *Education and mind in the knowledge age.* Mahwah, NJ: Erlbaum.

Bogatz, G. A., & Ball, S. (1971). *The second year of Sesame Street: A continuing evaluation.* Princeton, NJ: Educational Testing Service.

Bronfenbrenner, U. (1979). *The ecology of human development.* Cambridge, MA: Harvard University Press.

Brooks-Gunn, J., Duncan, G., & Aber, J. L. (Eds.). (1997). *Neighborhood poverty.* New York: Russell Sage Foundation.

Brown, J. S. (2000, March/April). Growing up digital. *Change,* 11–20.

Brown, J. S., Collins, A., & Duguid, P. (1989). Situated cognition and the culture of learning. *Educational Researcher, 18*(1), 32–42.

Bruner, J. (1977). *The process of education.* Cambridge, MA: Harvard University Press.

Bruner, J., Goodnow, J., & Austin, G. (1956). *A study of thinking.* New York: Wiley.

Bus, A., Van Ijzendoorn, M., & Pellegrini, A. (1995). Joint book reading makes for success in learning to read: A meta-analysis on intergenerational transmission of literacy. *Review of Educational Research, 65*(1), 1–21.

Chall, J., Jacobs, V., & Baldwin, L. (1990). *The reading crisis: Why poor children fall behind.* Cambridge, MA: Harvard University Press.

Chetty, R., Friedman, J., & Rockoff, J. (2012, April). The long-term impacts of teachers. Paper delivered at symposium. Columbia University, New York.

Chi, M., & Ceci, S. (1987). Content knowledge: Its role, representation, and restructuring in memory development. *Advances in Child Development and Behavior, 20*(1), 91–141.

Coiro, J., & Dobler, E. (2007). Exploring the comprehension strategies used by sixth-grade skilled readers as they search for and locate information on the Internet. *Reading Research Quarterly, 42*(2), 214–257.

Cole, M. (1990). *Cultural psychology.* Cambridge, MA: Belnap.

Connell, J. P., Kubisch, A., Schorr, L., & Weiss, C. (Eds.). (1995). *New approaches to evaluating community initiatives.* Washington, DC: The Aspen Institute.

Cook, T., Appleton, H., Conner, R., Shaffer, A., Tamkin, G., & Weber, S. (1975). *"Sesame Street" revisited.* New York: Russell Sage Foundation.

Cunningham, A., & Stanovich, K. (1991). Tracking the unique effects of print exposure in children: Associations with vocabulary, general knowledge, and spelling. *Journal of Educational Psychology, 83*(2), 264–274.

Cunningham, A., & Stanovich, K. (1998, Spring/Summer). What reading does for the mind. *American Educator, 22*(1), 8–15.

DeFleur, M., & Ball-Rokeach, S. (1989). *Theories of mass communication.* New York: Longmann.

Dewey, J. (1948). *Democracy and education: An introduction to the philosophy of education.* New York: Macmillan.

Dobbie, W., & Fryer, R. (2009). *Are high-quality schools enough to close the achievement gap? Evidence from a bold social experiment in Harlem.* Cambridge, MA: Harvard University.

Entwisle, D., Alexander, K., & Olson, L. S. (1997). *Children, schools, and inequality.* Boulder, CO: Westview.

Ericsson, K. A., Krampe, R. T., & Tesch-Romer, C. (1993). The role of deliberate practice in the acquisition of expert performance. *Psychological Review, 100*(3), 363–406.

Gelman, S., Coley, J., Rosengren, K., Hartman, E., & Pappas, A. (1998). Beyond labeling: The role of maternal input in the acquisition of richly structured categories. *Monographs of the Society for Research in Child Development* (vol. 63).

Glaser, R. (1984). Education and thinking: The role of knowledge. *American Psychologist, 39*(2), 93–104.

Goldsen, R. (1977). *The show and tell machine.* New York: Dial Press.

Goode, J., & Schneider, J. (1994). *Reshaping ethnic and racial relations in Philadelphia.* Philadelphia: Temple University Press.

Goodman, Y. (1984). The development of initial literacy. In H. Goelman, A. Oberg, & F. Smith (Eds.), *Awakening to literacy* (pp. 102–109). Exeter, NY: Heinemann.

Gough, P., & Tunmer, W. (1986). Decoding, reading, and reading disabilities. *Remedial and Special Education, 7*(1), 6–10.

Heyns, B. (1978). *Summer learning and the effects of schooling.* New York: Academic Press.

Hirsch, E. D. (1987). *Cultural literacy: What every American needs to know.* Boston, MA: Houghton-Mifflin.

Hirsch, E. D. (1996). *The schools we need and why we don't have them.* New York: Doubleday.

Jones, B. (2008). The knowledge trap: Human capital and development reconsidered. National Bureau of Economic Research Working Paper No. 14138.

Jones, B. (2009). The burden of knowledge and the "death of the renaissance man": Is innovation getting harder? *Review of Economic Studies, 76*(1), 283–317.

Kaefer, T., & Neuman, S. B. (2011, December). *A bi-directional relationship between conceptual organization and word learning.* Paper presented at the annual meeting of the Literacy Research Association, Jacksonville, FL.

Kahlenberg, R. (2001). *All together now.* Washington, DC: Brookings Institution Press.

Lareau, A. (2003). *Unequal childhoods.* Berkeley: University of California Press.

Leu, D., Kinzer, C., Coiro, J., & Cammack, D. (2000). The convergence of literacy instruction with networked technologies for information and communication. *Reading Research Quarterly, 35*(1), 108–127.

Levy, F., & Murnane, R. (2004). *The new division of labor: How computers are creating the next job market.* Princeton, NJ: Princeton University Press.

Lopez, S. (1994). *Third and Indiana.* New York: Penguin.

Mason, P. (2004). Annual income, hourly wages, and identity among Mexican-Americans and other Latinos. *Industrial Relations, 43*(4), 817–826.

Massey, D. (2007). *Categorically unequal.* New York: Russell Sage Foundation.

Massey, D., Gross, A., & Eggers, M. (1991). Segregation, the concentration of poverty, and the life chances of individuals. *Social Science Research, 20*(4), 397–420.

Massey, D., Gross, A., & Shibuya, K. (1994). Migration, segregation, and the geographic concentration of poverty. *American Sociological Review, 59*(3), 525–545.

Mayer, R. E. (2001). *Multimedia learning.* New York: Cambridge University Press.

McLaughlin, M., Irby, M., & Langman, J. (1994). *Urban sanctuaries.* San Francisco: Jossey-Bass.

Meier, D. (2002). *The power of their ideas.* Boston: Beacon Press.

Merton, R. (1948). The self-fulfilling prophesy. *The Antioch Review, 8*(2), 193–210.

Mol, S., Bus, A., deJong, M., & Smeets, D. (2008). Added value of dialogic parent-child book readings: A meta-analysis. *Early Education and Development, 19*(1), 7–26.

National Center for Education Statistics. (2000). *Teacher use of computers and the Internet in public schools.* Washington, DC: U.S. Department of Education, Office of Educational Research and Improvement.

National Early Literacy Panel. (2008). *Developing early literacy.* Washington, DC: National Institute for Literacy.

Neuman, S. B. (1995). *Literacy in the television age.* Norwood, CT: Ablex.

Neuman, S. B. (2009). The case for multimedia presentations in learning: A theory of synergy. In A. Bus & S. B. Neuman (Eds.), *Multimedia and literacy development: Improving achievement for young learners* (pp. 44–56). New York: Taylor & Francis.

Neuman, S. B., & Celano, D. (2006). The knowledge gap: Implications of leveling the playing field for low-income and middle-income children. *Reading Research Quarterly, 41*(2), 176–201.

Neuman, S. B., & Dwyer, J. (2011). Developing vocabulary and conceptual knowledge for low-income preschoolers: A design experiment. *Journal of Literacy Research, 43*(2), 103–129.

Neuman, S. B., Newman, E., & Dwyer, J. (2011). Educational effects of a vocabulary intervention on preschoolers' word knowledge and conceptual development: A cluster randomized trial. *Reading Research Quarterly, 46*(3), 249–272.

Neuman, S. B., & Roskos, K. (1993). Access to print for children of poverty: Differential effects of adult mediation and literacy-enriched play settings on environmental and functional print tasks. *American Educational Research Journal, 30*(1), 95–122.

Neuman, W. R. (Ed.). (2010). *Media, technology, and society.* Ann Arbor: University of Michigan Press.

Nisbett, R. (2009). *Intelligence and how to get it.* New York: W.W. Norton & Co.

Paivio, A. (2008). The dual coding theory. In S. B. Neuman (Ed.), *Educating the other America* (pp. 227–242). Baltimore, MD: Brookes.

Putnam, R. (2000). *Bowling alone: The collapse and revival of American community.* New York: Simon & Schuster.

Reardon, S. (2011). The widening academic achievement gap between the rich and the poor: New evidence and possible explanations. In G. Duncan & R. Murnane, *Whither opportunity* (pp. 91–116). New York: Russell Sage.

Recht, D., & Leslie, L. (1988). Effects of prior knowledge on good and poor readers' memory of text. *Journal of Educational Psychology, 80*(1), 16–20.

Rideout, V., Foehr, U., & Roberts, D. (2010). *GENERATION M2: Media in the lives of 8- to 18-year-olds.* Menlo Park, CA: Henry J. Kaiser Family Foundation.

Ross, L. (1977). The intuitive psychologist and his shortcomings: Distortions in the attribution process. In L. Berkowitz (Ed.), *Advances in experimental social psychology* (pp. 173–220). New York: Academic Press.

Rotherham, A., & Willingham, D. (2009). 21st century skills: The challenges that lie ahead. *Educational Leadership, 67*(1), 16–21.

Rumelhart, D. E. (1980). Schemata: The building blocks of cognition. In R. J. Spiro, B. C. Bruce, & W. F. Brewer (Eds.), *Theoretical issues in reading comprehension* (pp. 34–58). Hillsdale, NJ: Erlbaum.

Ryan, J. (2010). *Five miles away, a world apart.* New York: Oxford University Press.

Salomon, G. (1984). Television is "easy" and print is "tough": The differential investment of mental effort as a function of perceptions and attributions. *Journal of Educational Psychology, 76*(4), 647–658.

Scribner, S., & Cole, M. (1973). *The psychology of literacy.* Cambridge, MA: Harvard University Press.

Stanovich, K. E. (1986). Matthew Effects in reading: Some consequences of individual differences in the acquisition of literacy. *Reading Research Quarterly, 21*(4), 360–406.

Stanovich, K., & Cunningham, A. (1993). Where does knowledge come from? Specific associations between print exposure and information acquisition. *Journal of Educational Psychology, 85 (2),* 211–229.

Stanovich, K., West, R., & Harrison, M. (1995). Knowledge growth and maintenance across the life span: The role of print exposure. *Developmental Psychology, 31*(5), 811–826.

Stein, N., & Glenn, C. (1979). An analysis of story comprehension in elementary school children. In R. O. Freedle (Ed.), *Advances in discourse processing* (Vol. 2, pp. 53–120). Norwood, NJ: Ablex.

Walberg, H., & Tsai, S. (1983). Matthew Effects in education. *American Educational Research Journal, 20*(3), 359–373.

Whalen, C. (2001). *From Puerto Rico to Philadelphia: Puerto Rican workers and post war economies.* Philadelphia: Temple University Press.

Whitman, D. (2009). *Sweating the small stuff: Inner-city schools and the new paternalism.* Washington, DC: Thomas B. Fordham Institute.

Willingham, D. (2006). How knowledge helps. *American Educator, 30*(1), 1–12.

Willingham, D. (2010). Have technology and multi-tasking rewired how students learn? *American Educator, 34*(2), 23–28, 42.

Wilson, G., & Kelling, J. (1982). Broken windows. *The Atlantic, 104*(35), 8–10.

Wuchty, S., Jones, B., & Uzzi, B. (1997). The increasing dominance of teams in production of knowledge. *Science, 322*(5905), 1259–1262.

Index

Achievement First, 136
Adams, Marilyn, 53
Adults. *See also* Parents
  computer technology in libraries and,
    64–75, 94, 97–98
  importance of caring, 127–128
  librarians as "apostles of culture,"
    127–128
  reading activities of preschoolers and,
    45, 46–49, 56–57, 64–67
  reading activity of, 39–41, 56–57
Affordances, 22–23
African Americans. *See also names of*
  specific neighborhoods and neighborhood
  libraries
  in Chestnut Hill (Philadelphia), 10
  in Philadelphia Badlands, 13–14
  residential segregation of, 2, 13–14
After-school activities
  in Chestnut Hill (Philadelphia), 10,
    86–89
  in Philadelphia Badlands, 15, 84–88,
    97–98
Alber, J. L., 117
Alexander, Karl, 118
Alvarado, Tony, 133
Anchor charts, in Core Knowledge
  program, 141
Anderson, Dan, 84
Anderson, Elijah, 15
Appleton, H., 73
Arafeh, S., 84
Archer, John, 2
At-risk students, summer teen camp for,
  114–115
Austin, G., 112

Background knowledge, importance of,
  90, 99–100
Badlands. *See* Philadelphia Badlands
Baldwin, L., 77–78
Ball, S., 73
Ball-Rokeach, S., 76
Beentjes, J., 81, 88
Bereiter, C., 5
Bethune, Mary Macleod, 97
Blacks. *See* African Americans
Bogatz, G. A., 73
Bowman-Johnston, Kate, 54–55
Bronfenbrenner, Urie, 20, 53
Brooks-Gunn, J., 117
Brown, J. S., 108
Bruner, Jerome, 112
Bus, Adriana, 36, 49, 51

Cammack, D., 92
Carnegie libraries, 6, 17
Cashin, Kathleen, 140
Ceci, S., 107
Celano, Donna C., 19, 90
Center for Inquiry (New York City), 135
Chall, J., 77–78
Charter schools, 136–140
Chestnut Hill (Philadelphia). *See also*
  Chestnut Hill library
  after-school activities, 10, 86–89
  availability of print resources in,
    25–27, 29
  book access in preschool and
    elementary school, 33
  class segregation and, 9–11, 13
  comparison with Badlands, 13, 14, 15,
    17, 22–23, 38, 56, 120–122

comprehensive community-based
  initiative in, 15–21, 146–149
described, 9–11
ecological perspective on, 6–7
family income, 10
geographical isolation of, 8, 9–10, 13,
  22–23
history of, 9
impact of early access to print/
  reading, 36–37
map of, 8
need for economic integration,
  129–130
public school classroom libraries in,
  34, 35
raising children in, 10–11
reading and math scores in, 10
reading in public places, 28–32
residential segregation and, 22–23
street signs in, 24, 25, 26
summer programs, 109–113, 116
Chestnut Hill library. *See also* Chestnut
  Hill (Philadelphia)
adult reading activity in, 39–41, 56–57
comparison with Lillian Marero public
  library (Philadelphia Badlands),
  1–7, 38–57, 70–73, 121–122
concerted cultivation of reading and,
  48, 49
condition of books in, 35
described, 1, 17
homework of middle childhood
  students, 86–89
impact of access to computer
  technology, 59, 60–62, 67–73, 75,
  79–83, 87–89, 94–97, 100–103
importance of access to information,
  128–129
preschool reading activity in, 44–45,
  46–48, 50–55, 56–57
reading activities after introduction of
  computer technology, 61–62
reading activities prior to introduction
  of computer technology, 59–61
reading "up" or at grade level, 42–43
role of librarians, 127–128

users of, 2
William Penn Foundation initiative
  and, 16–17
young adult reading activity in, 41–43
Chetty, R., 131
Chi, M., 107
Chicago schools, Dewey in, 143
Child care
  in Chestnut Hill (Philadelphia), 10
  in Philadelphia Badlands, 14
China, postgraduate education in, 4
Churchill, Winston, 103
Class segregation, 2–5. *See also* Social
  stratification
  competition in areas of affluence, 56,
    69–70
  information capital and, 5–6
  Matthew effect and, 7, 18–20
  residential segregation and, 2–3, 9–11,
    13–14, 22–23
Coiro, J., 92, 93
Cole, M., 5, 36
Coley, J., 51
Collins, A., 108
Collins, P., 84
Community development initiative, of
  William Penn Foundation, 15–21,
  146–149
Competition
  in areas of affluence, 56, 69–70
  computers and, 75
Computer technology, 58–75. *See also*
  Internet
  adults and, 64–75, 94, 97–98
  at Chestnut Hill library, 59, 60–62,
    67–73, 75, 79–83, 87–89, 94–97,
    100–103
  in Chestnut Hill (Philadelphia)
    summer programs, 109–113
  frozen time checks and, 59–62
  importance of computer training and
    assistance, 127–128
  at Lillian Marero public library
    (Philadelphia Badlands), 58, 60,
    61–62, 64–67, 72, 73, 75, 79–83,
    88, 94–98, 102–104

Computer technology (*continued*)
  Matthew Effect and, 59, 75, 89
  new media and, 76–77, 79–83
  potential impact of, 76–77
  reading activities after introduction in
    public libraries, 59–62
  reading activities prior to introduction
    in public libraries, 59–61
  theory of displacement (Neuman) and,
    79–83
  video arcade role of, 66–67, 79
Connell, J. P., 16, 20
Conner, R., 73
Conscious reasoning, 5
Cook, Ann, 132
Cook, T., 73
Cooney, Joan Ganz, 73
Core Knowledge program, 140–143, 144
Cultural capital, 4
Cunningham, A., 5, 19, 49–51

DeFleur, M., 76
deJong, M., 49, 51
Dewey, John, 143
Digital divide. *See also* Level playing
    field concept
  access to computers and, 93–104
Displacement theory (Neuman), 79–83
Dobbie, W., 131
Dobler, E., 93
Duguid, P., 108
Duncan, G., 117
Dwyer, J., 51

Early Childhood Environment Rating Scale
    (ECERS), 32–33
Ecological systems theory
    (Bronfenbrenner), 53
Economic integration, need for,
    129–130
Eggers, M., 2
Engaging students, importance of, 129
Entwisle, Doris, 118
Environmental opportunity perspective,
    18–21
Ericsson, K. Anders, 107
Even Start, in Philadelphia Badlands, 14

Excellence School (Brooklyn, New
    York), 137
Excellence teachers, 136, 137
Expectations
  in Chestnut Hill versus Philadelphia
    Badlands, 123
  clarity of, 138
  Pygmalion effect, 115

Flipping, by preschoolers, 45–46, 53,
    64–65
Foehr, U., 101
Forbes.com, 10
Friedman, J., 131
Fryer, R., 131
Fundamental attribution error (Ross),
    3–4

Gang activity, in Philadelphia Badlands,
    13–15
Gelman, Susan, 51
Glaser, R., 107
Glenn, Christine, 36, 90
Goldsen, R., 73
Goode, J., 13
Goodman, Yetta, 24
Goodnow, J., 112
Gough, Philip, 62–63
Gross, A., 2, 15

Harrison, M., 19
Hartman, E., 51
Head Start, in Philadelphia Badlands,
    14, 51–52
Heyns, Barbara, 109
Hirsch, E. D., 5, 140–141
Hispanic Americans. *See* Latinos
Homework
  LEAP (after-school program), 84–88,
    97–98
  of middle childhood students, 83–91
  multitasking and, 84, 87, 88–89
Hooks, Benjamin, 87
Hughes, Langston, 3
Human capital
  cultural capital in, 4
  information capital in, 4–6, 105, 131

social capital in, 4
social geography in formation of, 3–4

India, postgraduate education in, 4
Inequity of educational opportunity
    access to computers and, 93–104
    access to print/reading and, 35–37
    role of material resources in, 38–39
Information capital, 4–6
    at Chestnut Hill library, 109–113, 117,
        118
    class segregation and, 5–6
    computer technology in formation of,
        108–119
    defined, 4–5
    development of, 5–6, 19, 89–90,
        106–119
    digital divide and, 93–104
    diminishing information-processing
        load and, 91
    expertise in development of, 106–111
    first-hand experience as source of
        information, 5
    Four C's for a global society, 106–107
    in human capital, 4–6, 105, 131
    impact of access to computer
        technology and, 79–81
    Internet in learning ecology of,
        108–119
    knowledge-based reasoning and, 5
    knowledge gap hypothesis (Neuman &
        Celano), 19, 20, 90–92, 118–119
    library role in providing, 16
    at Lillian Marero public library
        (Philadelphia Badlands), 109,
        113–117, 118
    Matthew Effect and, 90, 123
    mental power versus knowledge
        power in, 106–109
    policy recommendations for, 124–130
    print/reading as source of information,
        5
    research on development of, 6
    schemas and, 90–91
    transition from learning to read to
        reading to learn, 6–7, 77–78
Inquiry-based pedagogy, 133–134

Instructional scaffolding, 47, 74–75
Internet. *See also* Computer technology
    in development of information capital,
        108–119
    impact of access to computers and use
        of, 93–104, 113–116, 123–124
    motivational aspects of, 93
    specialized skills for using, 92, 93,
        97–102
    ubiquity of, 92–93
Irby, M., 127

Jacobs, V., 77–78
Johnson, Lyndon B., 73
Jones, B., 4, 105, 108

Kaefer, T., 51
Kahlenberg, R., 130
Kaiser Family Foundation, 101
Kelling, George, 137
King, Martin Luther, Jr., 144
Kinzer, C., 92
KIPP Academy (Bronx, New York),
    137–140
Klein, Joel, 142
Knowledge-based reasoning, 5
Knowledge deficit, 142
Knowledge gap hypothesis (Neuman &
    Celano), 19, 20, 90–92, 118–119
Knowledge networks, 90–91
Krampe, R. T., 107
Kravchak, Dunia, 87
Kubisch, A., 16, 20
Kumpf, Elaine, 86

Langman, J., 127
Lareau, A., 48
Latinos. *See also names of specific
    neighborhoods and neighborhood libraries*
    in Chestnut Hill (Philadelphia), 10
    in Philadelphia Badlands, 12–14
    residential segregation of, 2, 13–14
LEAP (after-school program), 84–88,
    97–98
LEGOTEXT, 111
Lenhart, A., 84
Leslie, Lauren, 90

Leu, D., 92
Level playing field concept, 7, 19–20,
    38–57
  impact of digital technology on,
    58–64, 73–75, 78–80
  paradox of, 42–43, 48–49, 56–57
  television and, 73–74
  "un-leveling" the playing field,
    124–125
Levin, D., 84
Levy, F., 4
Lillian Marero public library
    (Philadelphia Badlands). See also
    Philadelphia Badlands
  adult reading activity in, 39–41
  challenges of, 1, 2
  comparison with Chestnut Hill library,
    1–7, 38–57, 70–73, 121–122
  condition of books in, 35
  described, 1, 17
  forms of segregation and, 2–6
  homework of middle childhood
    students, 86, 88
  impact of access to computer
    technology, 58, 60, 61–62, 64–67,
    72, 73, 75, 79–83, 88, 94–98,
    102–104
  importance of access to information,
    128–129
  natural growth approach to reading
    and, 48–49
  preschool reading activity in, 44,
    45–46, 50, 52–53, 55–56
  preschool science activity, 116–117
  reading activities after introduction of
    computer technology, 61–62
  reading "down" in, 41–42, 43
  role of librarians, 127–128
  summer reading program, 113–116
  users of, 1–2, 3–4
  William Penn Foundation initiative
    and, 16–17
  young adult reading activity in, 41–43
Lopez, Steve, 13

Marrero, Lillian, 58

Mason, P., 2
Massey, Douglas, 2, 15
Mathematics, in Chestnut Hill
    (Philadelphia), 10
Matthew Effect
  access to computer technology and,
    59, 75, 89
  defined, 7, 18–20
  development of information capital
    and, 90, 123
  in environmental opportunity
    perspective, 18–20
Mayer, Richard E., 92–93
McLaughlin, Milbrey, 127
Meier, Deborah, 133, 136
Merton, Robert, 115
Middle childhood, 77–91
  homework as after-school activity,
    83–91
  LEAP (after-school program), 84–88
  reading and computer technology,
    78–83
  "simple view" language
    comprehension, 77–78
  transition from learning to read to
    reading to learn, 6–7, 77–78
  vocabulary development, 78
"Miracle" schools, 132–136
Mol, S., 49, 51
Multitasking
  asynchronous/synchronous, 87
  homework and, 84, 87, 88–89
Murnane, R., 4

National Academies of Sciences, 20
National Assessment of Educational
    Progress (NAEP), 137
National Center for Education Statistics,
    94
National Early Literacy Panel, 49
Natural growth approach to reading,
    48–49
Neuman, Susan B., 18, 19, 51, 81, 90,
    92, 131
Neuman, W. R., 92
New Jersey Growers Association, 12

New literacies, 92–104
    access to computers and, 93–104
    defining, 92
    reading demands of, 92, 93, 98–102
    ubiquity of Internet and, 92–93
Newman, E., 51
New York Times, 142
Nisbett, R., 106
North Philadelphia East, 14
Nye, Bill, 116

Ogbu, John, 122
Olson, L. S., 118
Operation Sunrise, 13

Paivio, Allan, 92–93
Palmer, Sara, 55–56
Pappas, A., 51
Parents. *See also* Adults
    computer technology in libraries and,
        64–75
    in concerted cultivation of reading,
        48, 49
    importance of parent involvement
        training, 125–127
    in natural growth approach to reading,
        48–49
    of preschool readers, 45, 46–49
    shared book reading and, 49–53
Paternalism schools, 136–140
Pellegrini, A., 36
Philadelphia Badlands. *See also* Lillian
    Marero public library (Philadelphia
    Badlands)
    after-school activities, 15, 84–88, 97–98
    availability of print resources in,
        27–28
    book access in preschool and
        elementary school, 33
    class segregation and, 13–15
    comparison with Chestnut Hill, 13, 14,
        15, 17, 22–23, 38, 56, 120–122
    comprehensive community-based
        initiative in, 15–21, 146–149
    computer technology and hope for
        level playing field, 58–64, 73–75

described, 1, 11–15
    ecological perspective on, 6–7
    family income, 14
    gang activity in, 13–15
    geographical isolation of, 8, 22–23
    history of, 12–13
    impact of early access to print/
        reading, 36–37
    map of, 8
    need for economic integration,
        129–130
    public school classroom libraries in,
        34, 35
    raising children in, 13–15
    reading and math scores in, 14
    reading in public places, 29–32
    residential segregation and, 2–3, 9–11,
        13–14, 22–23
    street signs in, 24–25, 26
    summer programs, 113–116
Poverty. *See also* Lillian Marero public
    library (Philadelphia Badlands);
    Philadelphia Badlands
    dependence on school to increase
        achievement, 52–53, 109, 116–117
    impact on children and families, 117,
        118
    need for economic integration,
        129–130
    residential segregation and, 2–3, 9–11,
        13–14, 22–23
Preschoolers
    access to technology, 58, 64–73
    competition among, 69–70
    early reading skills development,
        44–57, 64–65, 126–127
    "flipping" by, 45–46, 53, 64–65
    parental approach to reading and,
        48–49
    reading activity of, 44–57
    relationship between word learning
        and conceptual development,
        51–53
    science activity of, 116–117
    shared book reading and, 49–53
Print/reading. *See* Reading

Prior knowledge, importance of, 90, 99–100
P.S. 254 (Queens, New York), 140–143
Purposeful talk, in Core Knowledge program, 142
Putnam, R., 4
Pygmalion effect, 115

Quality teachers, impact on students, 131

Rainie, L., 84
Rathmann, Peggy, 2
Reading
  access in preschools and elementary schools, 32–33
  adult reading activity, 39–41, 56–57
  availability of print resources, 23, 25–28, 29, 31–32
  in building information capital, 5–6
  Carnegie libraries and, 6, 17
  computer role in building skills, 73–75
  demands of new literacies, 92, 93, 98–102
  early reading skills development, 44–57, 64–65, 126–127
  environmental features and, 29–33
  impact of summer academic programs, 118–119
  importance of, 5
  inequity of educational opportunity and, 35–37
  after introduction of computers in public libraries, 59–62
  in knowledge acquisition, 19–20
  parental impact on early reading achievement, 36
  prior to introduction of computers in public libraries, 59–61
  in public places, 28–32
  public school classroom libraries and, 33–35
  simple view of learning to read, 62–64, 77–78
  skills needed for online, 92, 93, 97–102

as source of information, 5
street signs, 24–25, 26
summer programs, 113–116
transition from learning to read to reading to learn, 6–7, 77–78
young adult reading activity, 41–43
Reading wars, 143
Reardon, S., 2
Recht, Donna, 90
Rideout, V., 101
Roberts, D., 101
Rockoff, J., 131
Rosengren, K., 51
Rosetta Stone software, 3
Roskos, K., 18
Ross, L., 4
Rotherham, A., 105
Rule-based reasoning, 5
Rumelhart, Donald E., 90
Russia, postgraduate education in, 4
Ryan, J., 2

Salomon, Gabriel, 81
Sanford, John, 2
Scarry, Richard, 45
Schemas, 90–91
Schneider, J., 13
Schorr, L., 16, 20
Scribner, S., 5, 36
Segregation, 2–6
  Black, 2, 13–14
  class. See Class segregation
  hyper-segregation, 2
  Latino, 2, 13–14
  residential, 2–3, 9–11, 13–14, 22–23
Self-fulfilling prophecy, 115
Self-regulation, 139–140
Shaffer, A., 73
Shibuya, K., 15
Signs, street, 24–25, 26
Silicon Valley phenomenon, 108–109
Simple view of learning to read, 62–64, 77–78
Smeets, D., 49, 51
Social capital, 4

Social networking, impact on writing
  skills, 98–99
Social stratification, 22–37. *See also* Level
  playing field concept; Matthew
  Effect
  comparison of Philadelphia Badlands
    and Chestnut Hill, 22–23, 56
  defining, 22
  impact of, 22
  impact on parents' approaches to
    reading, 48–49, 56
  of information capital, 19, 56
Stanovich, Keith E., 5, 18, 19, 49–51
Stein, Nancy, 36, 90
Stetson Hat Factory, 12, 13
Story grammars, 90
Story-time hour, 48
Street signs, 24–25, 26
Summer programs
  Chestnut Hill (Philadelphia), 109–113,
    116
  impact of summer academic
    programs, 118–119
  Philadelphia Badlands, 113–116

Tamkin, G., 73
Teachers
  excellence, 136, 137
  expectations for students, 115, 138
  quality, impact on students, 131
  self-fulfilling prophesy and, 115
Television
  displacement of homework activities,
    84
  level playing field and, 73–74
  as passive medium, 81–83
  schemas on, 90
  theory of displacement (Neuman) and,
    79–83
Temple University, 20, 109–111
Tesch-Romer, C., 107
Theory of displacement (Neuman),
  79–83
Third and Indiana (Lopez), 13

ThisIBelieve.org, 101
Timothy Academy, 114
Transfer schools, 132–135
Tsai, Shio-Ling, 18
Tunmer, William, 62–63
Tweens. *See* Middle childhood

Unequal Childhood (Lareau), 48
Urban Academy Laboratory School
  (New York City), 132–135, 136, 140,
  143
Uzzi, B., 108

Van der Voort, T., 88
Van Ijzendoorn, C., 36
Viorst, Judith, 2
Vocabulary development, 52–53, 78,
  89–90, 99–100

Walberg, Herb, 18
War on Poverty, 16, 73
Webb, Steve, 54
Weber, S., 73
Weiss, C., 16, 20
West, R., 19
Whalen, Carmen, 12–13
White flight, 13
Whitman, D., 136
William Penn Foundation
  comprehensive community
    development and, 15–21, 146–149
  environmental opportunity
    perspective and, 18–21
  evaluating initiative of, 20–21
  libraries and comprehensive
    community development
    initiative, 16–17, 59, 122–124
  policy implications of research,
    124–130
Willingham, Daniel, 5, 87, 105
Wilson, James, 137
Wuchty, Stefan, 108

Young adults, reading activity of, 41–43

About the Authors

Susan B. Neuman is a professor of Educational Studies specializing in early literacy development. Previously, she has served as the U.S. Assistant Secretary for Elementary and Secondary Education. In her role as assistant secretary, she established the Early Reading First program, developed the Early Childhood Educator Professional Development Program, and was responsible for all activities in Title I of the Elementary and Secondary Act. She has directed the Center for the Improvement of Early Reading Achievement (CIERA) and currently directs the Michigan Research Program on Ready to Learn. She has served on the IRA Board of Directors (2001–2003) and other numerous boards of nonprofit organizations. Along with Linda Gambrell, she is the incoming editor of *Reading Research Quarterly*, the most prestigious journal in reading research. Her research and teaching interests include early childhood policy, curriculum, and early reading instruction, preK–grade 3 for children who live in poverty. She has written over 100 articles and authored and edited 11 books, including *The Handbook of Early Literacy Research* (Volumes I, II, & III) with David Dickinson, *Changing the Odds for Children at Risk* (Teachers College Press, 2009), *Educating the Other America* (2008), and *Multimedia and Literacy Development* (2008).

Donna C. Celano, Ph.D., is currently assistant professor of Communication at La Salle University in Philadelphia, where she teaches courses in mass media and media research methods. Previously, she served as assistant professor of Communication at Chestnut Hill College, Philadelphia. She received a Ph.D. in communication from Temple University in Philadelphia. Donna's research focuses on low- and middle-income children's access and use of information resources. Previous projects include research on computer availability for children in low-income neighborhoods; the "Major Libraries Urban Grant," a study of branch library renovations and their influences on children's access to books and technology; and "Books Aloud," a "book flood," incorporating parent education and teacher training in Philadelphia child care centers. Her research has appeared recently in *Educational Leadership*, *Teachers College Record*, and *Phi Delta Kappan*.